WIVES LEADING

WIVES LEADING

AN UNUSUAL BOOK ON BIBLICAL LEADERSHIP

RICK THOMAS

WIVES LEADING:
An Unusual Book on Biblical Leadership

ISBN 978-1-7323854-7-4

Rick Thomas

© 2025 Life Over Coffee

Unless otherwise noted, all Scripture references herein are from the English Standard Version, copyright © 2001 by Crossway, Inc. Used by permission. All rights reserved.

No part of this publication may be reproduced, stored in a retrieval system, or transmitted in any form or by any means without the express written permission of Life Over Coffee.

Edited by Sarah Hayhurst

Life Over Coffee
8595 Pelham Rd Ste 400 #406,
Greenville, SC 29615
LifeOverCoffee.com

Brothers, if anyone is caught in any transgression, you who are spiritual should restore him in a spirit of gentleness. Keep watch on yourself, lest you too be tempted. Bear one another's burdens, and so fulfill the law of Christ. For if anyone thinks he is something, when he is nothing, he deceives himself.
(Galatians 6:1–3)

For additional resources, visit
lifeovercoffee.com

Table of Contents

    Introduction 8
1. An Effective Wife 14
2. The Critical Wife 22
3. Unique Couple 30
4. See No Problem 40
5. An Imperfect Person 50
6. How to Be Honest 58
7. Setting Aside 66
8. Immature Husband 76
9. Power of Unforgiveness 84
10. Need to Forgive 92
11. A Harsh Husband 100
12. Disciple and Submit 108
13. Leading Practically 116
14. Over Your Head 124
    Conclusion 132
    About the Author 137

Introduction

With the Lord on the point of the home, the husband becomes the subordinate leader of the home, and after the husband is his wife. The children orient themselves under their parents as they humbly submit and follow the parents' God-centered examples. Because the wife has two roles, there is a "double dependency" regarding how she relates to her husband and God. In one sense, she submits to her husband and depends on him in limited ways while her ultimate authority is God Almighty. Every wife is double-dependent.

Follow Us As We Follow Christ

Her double dependency does not negate her equality with her husband. She is equal to her husband as she submits to him. Though she is a coequal image bearer of God, it is incumbent upon her to submit and respond well to her husband's leadership and care. I realize this worldview creates tension and even anger among some wives because the Bible's ideal is not their lived experience. I understand, but human failure should not alter God's plan for our marriages. Perhaps thinking through inferior models for the home will encourage you to seek God's solutions over fallen variations.

- Parents who orient their home to serve the children primarily.
- Husbands who orient themselves around their wives or their children rather than God.
- Wives who orient themselves around their children instead of their husbands.
- A husband who is passive in his relationship with God.
- A wife who is bitter toward her husband.

Proper biblical orientation of the home should look like a husband in vigorous pursuit of God, a wife who humbly follows him, and the children who come along in the wake of the parents' leadership. This dynamic creates biblical, familial success. Anything else will lead the family into chaos, even leading to generational complications.

Orientation Breakdown

This conversation nearly always stirs one question: "What if my husband is not humbly and passionately following the Lord?" It is a relevant and sad question because many Christian husbands do not biblically lead their wives and children. I live in the real world where fallenness is all around us. To expect everyone to attain the aims of Scripture is naive. A husband's lack of biblical leadership can be frustrating for a wife. It is also a challenging counseling situation when a wife is willing to submit to her husband, but he does not desire to fulfill his role of leading the family by passionately and wisely pursuing God.

In these sad cases, the wife still has a biblical leader who will help her: she can continue to submit to the Lord. If her husband refuses to lead her biblically, she can experience biblical leadership from God. The same perspective applies to the children. It took me a long time to realize this beautiful truth. I spent the first two decades of my life angry because those who were supposed to lead me—my parents—did not lead me well. Rather than submitting my heart to the Lord, I chose anger, victimization, and justifications for the misery that I was experiencing.

Their lack of gospel adherence should not have had so much power over my mind and behaviors. They did not make me sin in response to their nonsensical parenting; I chose to sin as I donned the role of a helpless victim. After relinquishing my desire for a better home life, I found freedom through the grace of God. I let go of what they would not give me and grabbed what the Lord offered. If you are sinfully angry toward anyone for what they have done or not done, you will never be free from their control over you, and you will never experience what the Lord is willing to give you despite what others have done to you. If this is you, I appeal to you to let go of what you are not getting and begin pleading with the Lord to fill this emptiness in your life.

Introduction

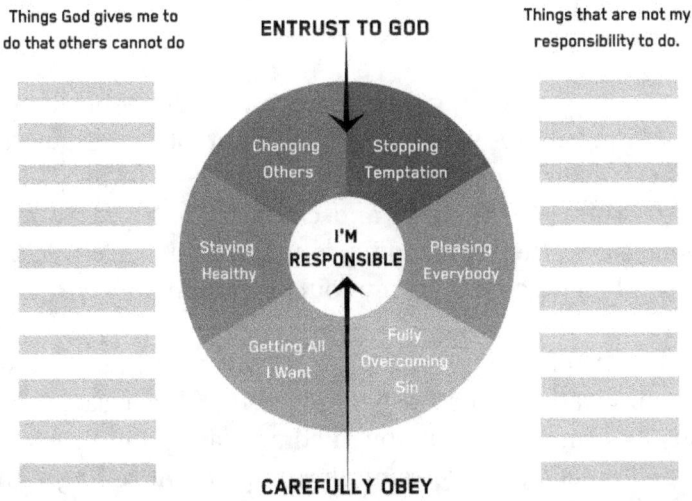

First Five

STEP ONE: Confess to the Lord how your good desire for a better situation has made you bitter, angry, cynical, fearful, or possibly anxious. Pick all that apply while adding others that more accurately describe your heart's condition. Plead with our good Lord to remove this sin from your heart (1 John 1:8–10).

STEP TWO: Ask Him to bring contentment, even in an undesirable relationship (2 Corinthians 12:7–10). To do this, you must identify what you're not getting from your husband or how he's a disappointment. Please recognize that your desires are probably wholesome, like proper leadership.

STEP THREE: These hidden idolatries will mainly circle around fear and anger. You're afraid of what might happen if he continues not to lead, or you're angry that he won't

11

lead and how his lack adds to your responsibility to do your job and his too.

Step Four: Find a friend of the same gender to become a mentor to care for you, hold you accountable, and spur you on to love and good deeds (Hebrews 10:24–25). This person must exhibit compassion and courage. If they only have compassion, they will coddle you. You do not need that. If they only have courage, they could be unkind.

Step Five: Tenaciously work to renew your mind. Your sin is complicating your husband's sin. I did not say you're causing him to sin, but you're complicating the problems in the home. It's like the sinfully angry parent yelling at the child for being angry. First, the parents must repent of their sin before they can help the children.

Call to Action

1. If you're disappointed with your husband's leadership, will you admit that you might sabotage what God could do through you? Reflect on the illustration of the angry parent trying to help an angry child. Is there something you should do to resolve this problem? If so, please take those steps.
2. What one thing will you change about yourself to begin the reorientation of your home? How will you lead your husband from a place of biblical submission?
3. Who will you talk to each time you fail in this leadership opportunity? You will fail; we all do. It would be best if you had someone who won't coddle you or be harsh but would courageously guide you through repentance so you can get back to helping your family.
4. Do you think it's unfair for you to be a double-dependent wife? Why do you believe that? What about everyone else who lives within a hierarchy while submitted to God and others? What about a child who is double-dependent? Is it wrong to depend upon his parents and God too? How would you guide a child who had awful parents? Perhaps applying that advice to you will help you as you lead your husband from a submitted position.

1

An Effective Wife

One of the most critical questions a wife could ask herself is how she compares herself to her husband. Is she better, worse, or similar to her husband? How she thinks about her role in her marriage and relationship with her husband will determine the trajectory of the union, for good or bad. I'm assuming—for this discussion—that both spouses are maturing, humble, and willing to communicate on the level this perspective requires. If one or both partners are pulling against each other, what I have to say here will not apply. So, back to my question: how do you compare yourself to your husband?

Paul answered the "how I compare myself to you" question in 1 Timothy 1:15 when he said he was the most significant sinner he knew. Paul's self-assessment flies in the face of our self-esteem culture, which cannot handle this kind of biblical ego chastening. The irony is how Paul's view of himself is an honest, hope-filled assessment that leads to personal freedom and relational harmony. It is honest because the biblical record is clear—we are unworthy sinners who put Christ on the cross (Romans 3:10–12). It is hope-filled because Christ came to free sinners from captivity (Luke 19:10). Humble admissions to the reality of who we are is the only way we will experience rescue from who we are (James 4:6).

Paul was not discouraged by how he thought about

himself. His healthy view became a robust platform upon which he could love God and others most effectively, a platform a wife should construct to help her husband mature into a God-honoring leader. If she understands how what she did to Christ is far worse than anything anyone has done to her, she will position herself as a powerful means of effectual grace in her husband's life. You see this idea in Matthew 18:32–33:

> Then his master summoned him and said to him, "You wicked servant! I forgave you all that debt because you pleaded with me. And should not you have had mercy on your fellow servant, as I had mercy on you?"

The person that the master was talking to had more significant debt than the fellow he was beating up, but the master released the greater debtor. His question—should not you have had mercy on your fellow servant, as I had compassion on you?—is practically relevant for all of us. We can practicalize it by asking—from our perspective—who is the most prominent sinner we know? From Paul's perspective, it was him. From my perspective, it is me. What about you? Who is the biggest sinner that you know—from your perspective? I trust you would argue Paul and me down from our chief sinner seats, recognizing that you are the chief of all the sinners.

Sin Comparing

If we are convinced our sin against God is more significant than anything ever done to us, there is no reason for us to be sinful toward others. Even if we cannot transact forgiveness because the offender is not asking, we should have an attitude of forgiveness toward those who have sinned against us (Luke 23:34) while hoping God will grant repentance to them

(2 Timothy 2:24–25) so we can transactionally forgive them. An attitude of forgiveness spills out of the chief sinner's heart, becoming the antidote that keeps him from criticalness, bitterness, anger, and other spiteful characteristics from sabotaging his soul. We can have this attitude if we have the correct view of ourselves. To withhold a heart of pity and forgiveness from someone who has sinned against us denies the gospel we say we love (Romans 2:4, 5:8). Unkindness transgresses gospel lines (Ephesians 4:29).

We become idolatrous whenever we step outside biblical boundaries to acquire something we want. Idolatry is an attitude of the heart that acts sinfully to satisfy unrighteous desires. For example, a child wants a toy. It's not an evil desire, but his parent does not give him the toy. The child throws a temper tantrum until the parent consents. The attitude of the child's heart turned evil because what he wanted was more important than honoring or respecting a fellow image-bearer. The child's behavior too often happens in marriages, and a wife is particularly susceptible, especially if her husband is not learning, loving, or leading her according to her "biblical" expectations. The blindside is that her desire for a biblical marriage is appropriate, proper, and something she should expect.

Good desires not met put the wife on dangerous ground because she is a hairsbreadth from falling into the unmet desires trap. Suppose she does not appropriate God's power to her unmet biblical desires. It will only be a matter of time before she becomes critical, bitter, resentful, cynical, harsh, unkind, and full of regret. She will need to do significant soul work, which starts with a robust self-assessment of who she is in light of the gospel's narrative. For example, is she quicker to let herself off the hook than her husband? A common problem is glossing over our sins while lingering long over the sins of others. The temptation is that when a person does not get what they want, they will elevate the unmet craving over any self-righteous judgments or sinful reactions toward the person who did not come through for them. They are playing a dangerous sin-comparing game.

> Not that we dare to classify or compare ourselves with some of those who are commending themselves. But when they measure themselves by one another and compare themselves with one another, they are without understanding.
> (2 Corinthians 10:12)

> The Pharisee, standing by himself, prayed thus: "God, I thank you that I am not like other men."
> (Luke 18:11)

Sinning Victims

Suppose we do not see ourselves as similar in kind to others—from an Imago Dei perspective. In that case, we will elevate ourselves above those who disappoint us (James 3:9). No matter how disappointing the other person is, no one is better than anyone else. There is no biblical warrant to look down on another person. Self-righteousness is the heart condition that exalts superior attitudes toward others. God does not bless these attitudes (James 4:6). To sin against someone in response to their sin reveals a person's adverse, albeit authentic, walk with Jesus while creating an awkward dualism with the person they sinned against in the relationship. This dualism is the sinning victim construct. There are few discipling situations more challenging than the sinning victim. It happens too often.

For example, a wife shares how her husband sinned against her and her sinful responses to him. He has sinned against her, making her a victim. She sins against him in response, making her a sinner. It is a delicate process as you walk her through what is wrong with the marriage. Part of the problem is her culpability in the deterioration of the marriage. You cannot move too fast with this knowledge because she will misunderstand you, perceiving you as harsh with your accusation and assuming you do not recognize what her husband did to her. Thus, you begin by carefully understanding her suffering while sympathetically listening to the hurt and fears she has experienced. Her pain is real. Her story is dark.

More than likely, she is correct: her husband has been mean and insensitive toward her. You must give her appropriate time and space to weep over and work through the disappointment that has characterized their marriage (Romans 12:15). You do not want to prematurely introduce more tension into the narrative by addressing her guilt until you have competently, compassionately, and thoroughly communicated your care for her (Romans 8:31). You want to slowly bring her to the place where she can hear the whole truth about what is wrong with their covenant. Your ultimate goal is to position her heart to receive God's help, not just fix her husband.

- She needs to know the Lord is not oblivious to what is happening in her marriage.
- She needs to know God is for her, and He has a better plan for their marriage.
- She needs to know there is no problem where God's grace is inadequate to repair it.
- She needs to know the Lord can use the sin in their marriage to redeem their marriage.

Choose Freedom

These good things can happen if she grieves over the disorderedness in his soul and their marriage while taking her soul to task by fixing what she can about herself. You want her to grieve but not fall into despair. You want her to correct unbiblical thinking but not crush her spirit

(Isaiah 42:3; Matthew 12:20). The most common question about this process is, "How do I do this?" The first step is to ensure she is not complicating the problem through personal sinfulness. As you do this, you must discern how God desires to guide you (John 16:13) while trusting Him to work through you to restore her as the precursor to working on what's wrong with him.

If she is going to be a gentle restorer of her husband, she must keep watch over her soul, ensuring the evil one has not entrapped her (Galatians 6:1–3). Don't assume she is ready to be part of God's restoration team when sin is harboring in her heart. It would help if you also let her know that they will not likely simultaneously repent during this season. Their marriage is not a happily-ever-after movie. It's real life. Scriptwriters do not factor in how the doctrine of sin practically works out in our lives. They are making movies, but in real life, every story does not end according to how you want it. We are not in control of the narrative (2 Corinthians 1:8–9). Sin is messy, and there will be times when things do not end with everyone smiling, hugging, and heading over the horizon as the sun fades to black.

Families do divide. Marriages do fail. Christ experienced crucifixion (Isaiah 53:10). Counseling does not assure preferred outcomes. The husband may never become what the wife wants (2 Corinthians 12:8–9). This potential is where the wife of an unchanging man needs gospel clarity. The gospel can give her what she needs to find restoration, and it can give her all she needs to live in an unreconciled situation with her husband (2 Peter 1:3). There are two options for her. If her husband does not repent, will she forgive him attitudinally? If her husband does repent, will she forgive him transactionally? Attitudinal forgiveness is about her heart's attitude toward him; perchance he does not change. She does not want his unrepentant sin to manage her. Thus, the best she can do is free herself from his sin. She can be free even if he never chooses to be free.

No Curve Here

The challenge in an unchanging marriage is whether the "victim" will do the work to guard his or her heart against being a sinful, self-righteous person. God does not grade on a curve. Nobody receives special favor from God as though one person is better than someone else; we're all rotten to the core and require the Lord's favor (Isaiah 64:6). There are only two grades of people. The Father gives us an F-. He gives His Son an A+. I was a depraved human that God regenerated by grace (Romans 3:12). My good fortune did not come because I turned over a new leaf and became a good person. My redemption and ongoing restoration to God is an undeserved gift from Him (Ephesians 2:8–10). I have no right to think my effort makes me better than anyone. If my works are good, it is because God works through me. He is good. Paul could not be more explicit:

> None is righteous, no, not one; no one understands; no one seeks for God. All have turned aside; together they have become worthless; no one does good, not even one.
>
> (Romans 3:10–12)

We cannot grade each other on a curve to feel better about ourselves while belittling others. We are bad to the bone. We are simultaneously sinners and victims. Though some sins are consequentially worse than others, we must recognize that any sin is significant enough to put Christ on the cross (James 2:10). This kind of gospel-informed thinking releases us from being controlled by the sins of others, especially by disappointing people who never change.

If you understand and practically apply these truths, you will be positioned in the best possible place to help your spouse overcome the things that disrupt your marriage. I'm not saying your spouse will change, but you can rise above the fray by living a gospel-centered life that recognizes that God made both of you in the Imago Dei. It's never right to sin in response to sin. You can forgive in your heart regardless of what the other person does, and with a spirit of humility, you're in the best place to courageously and compassionately confront, correct, care for, and compel your spouse to change their ways. If they do not choose to change, you will have no regret because you've done all that depends on you to be the most effective spouse you can be (Romans 12:18).

Call to Action

1. Do you pity your spouse as a fallen fellow sinner needing God's empowering favor? If not, why not?
2. Though the consequences for sin can differ significantly, why is it essential to see all humans as equal sinners, standing at the foot of the cross?
3. Why would Paul say he was the foremost sinner at the end of his life, knowing others have committed more numerous and grievous sins than him?
4. Why are good desires we don't get from our spouses so deceptive, even tempting us to sin in response to not getting that thing from our spouses?
5. How are you responding to your unchanging spouse? Do you need to treat him differently when he disappoints you? What specific and practical ways will you change?

2

The Critical Wife

Proverbs says that death and life are in the power of the tongue, and those who love it will eat its fruits. The wisdom of Proverbs teaches how we will eat the fruit of our words, whether our words are good or bad. This truth can be particularly biting for the wife with a husband who does not fulfill God's mandate to lead her well. Her temptation is to be critical. She needs God's grace to help her live a submitted life that overcomes his deficiencies while not disparaging him with her words. It's a tall order, but there is grace for this.

Adam's Instincts

> Know this, my beloved brothers: let every person be quick to hear, slow to speak, slow to anger; for the anger of man does not produce the righteousness of God.
>
> (James 1:19–20)

James had a lot to say about the tongue. The third chapter of his letter is devoted to it, but before he went into a fuller treatment about this little member, he gave us some insight at the beginning of his letter. He said that a person's anger does not produce a righteous lifestyle. The implication is clear: if you want someone to mature in Christ, sinful anger is not how to get them there—no matter what they did to you. For example, Mable wants Biff to be a more considerate husband—a good desire that any loving wife should have for her husband.

Of course, her biblical desire does not negate her biblical duty. Mable must recognize her responsibility in Biff's ongoing discipleship. She has a coequal obligation in their one-flesh conjugal adventure. His failures do not relieve Mable of the admonition to lead well by displaying Christ in their home. We all know that no one is permitted to sin in response to someone's sin. However, we see this regularly in today's culture. Someone legitimately sins against another person, and the offended party does something reprehensible in retaliation to the person who offended them.

We deplore and decry these things, but too often, we do similar things in our marriages. Maybe we don't perceive our offenses in such light because marriage mishaps are not as consequentially devastating as our culture's violent retaliations. In God's eyes, it's a different matter. Though consequence vary, any sin—big or small—puts Christ on the cross. The Father punished His Son for all our lesser marital transgressions too. Ignoring little offenses, especially those that roll off our tongues, would be a substantial marital mistake. But how easy is it to sin against our spouses with our words? When they disappoint us, our Adamic instincts override biblical common sense, and we are no longer quick to hear and slow to speak.

How to Speak

Mable will have some serious and challenging heart work before she can position herself to help her husband. Biff is sinning against her. It's objective and offensive. She cannot disregard what he's doing or her responsibility to assist because her body is rejecting her body—they are one flesh. It's a spiritual-marital disease when a part of our body attacks another part. Paul gave us insight on how to cooperate with the Lord in the process of helping an offending person change (1 Corinthians 3:6). Mable will have to employ Paul's wisdom. In Romans 2:4, Paul calls her to use the encouragement method to motivate him to change, and in Ephesians 4:29, he appeals to her to use her tongue redemptively to build up her husband.

Being an encourager or uplifter of a careless person is especially hard if the negligent person has been neglecting you for years. And that is how it usually goes. Most of my marriage counseling on this level happens after the marriage has been deteriorating for a decade or more. It is rare for a couple to ask for counseling after their first year or two to tweak a few things they see going south. Most marriages muddle along until someone can't take it any longer, but by then, they are at the grenade launching stage, not the soft answer stage.

Mable has a tough job. The marriage has gone wrong for too long, and she needs to say something. The question is not whether Mable should critique and correct her husband but how she should do it. Her opportunity is where she will have to examine her criticisms and corrections. What is motivating her to speak to Biff? Jesus said our words are the secondary focus while the motivation for our words is the primary thing (Luke 6:45). Mable needs to examine her heart attitude for Biff before she speaks to him. She must heed James' warning: a person's anger does not produce the righteousness of God. If anger is in her heart, it will assuredly come out of her mouth.

Friends Change Friends

In another place, James gave insight on identifying anger when he said that you find anger's source in our passions, desires, and coveting (James 4:1–2). This happens when a person like Mable blinds herself to her approach to her husband. She can want him to change so badly that she forgets how to approach him, especially when her ticking heart is ticked off. There is corruption in her excellent desire for a better marriage. Our most destructive conversations can happen when we know we're right. Mable is right. She knows she's right: Biff needs to change. We see this in our culture too. So many things need to change, which can blind us to the wrongness of the methods we employ to bring change.

> Faithful are the wounds of a friend.
> (Proverbs 27:6)

It is rare for adversaries to stop being adversaries. The most effective change occurs among friends. Right now, Mable is not Biff's authentic friend. She is angry with him. She might say something trite like, "I love him, but I don't like him." That is deceptive semantics that soothes the conscience but is devastating for the marriage. If Mable does not perceive and change her attitude toward her husband, her words will not produce righteousness in him. She must plant the gospel firmly in her mind. It would be easy for her to enter the "why me" mode. "Why should I be the one to change first when he has been such a jerk for so long?" It's a valid complaint, but there is only one correct answer: God calls us to carry our crosses as we follow the example of Jesus.

And don't forget that our sin put Him on the tree. He had to make the first move because we could not move (Ephesians 2:1). Christ, the offended, reached out to us, the offenders. Amazing grace! Someone in this marriage will have to set aside their preferences for the greater good of the marriage (Philippians 2:5–6). To ask Biff to be mature when he has not shown any signs of maturity for a decade or more is unrealistic. It would be great if he suddenly got a clue, but that rarely happens. It didn't occur to me when

I needed Christ to act upon me. It didn't happen to you. It probably won't happen with Biff. It will be on Mable to cooperate with God to make the first mature move in their marriage. She will have to be the Christlike leader. She will have to die first.

Divine Affection

Mable must take her heart to task regarding her affection for Biff. She must plead with God to give her grace for her annoying husband. She must let the gospel be her guide: Jesus loved annoying Mable so much that He died for her (Romans 5:8). As she is begging God to change her hurt heart, she must find a better place to begin helping Biff. She will likely not be able to start with her most grave disappointment. Too often, a spouse will bring up her biggest annoyance about the marriage. Usually, that is too much truth for the historically proven unchanging person to respond to so he can change.

It's similar to debt reduction. It's typically more effective to start with smaller debts before you tackle the larger ones. If Biff is immature and has a proven record of not changing, bringing up his most challenging sin is probably a bad idea. I'm not talking about sins like adultery or other devastating addictive behaviors. I'm talking about "over-look-able" things like passivity, poor communication habits, inability to prioritize Biff's life, messiness, not considering Mable, lack of passion for Jesus, and fear-motivated inhibitions. Newly married couples often make this mistake: now that they are married, they anticipate how the other spouse will be all they had dreamed of them being.

The boyfriend wooed her off her feet, and she floated down the aisle. That should be the beginning of the "happily ever after" storyline. Back to Earth: Most of these couples enter marriage without a sin plan, and as the little disappointments mount, they develop poor ways of dealing with them until they become Biff and Mable. Biff did not stop being a work-in-progress on his wedding day. Neither did Mable. After the marital dust settled, they should have seen their joint brokenness and need for ongoing mutual care. It's like the marriage dust settled in their eyes, blinding them. Mable will have to set aside—as much as she possibly can—what's wrong with Biff. She will have to help him grow.

Growth Areas

These areas of growth must be reachable goals. Mable must be his caring and courageous cheerleader. With enough work, some of the more significant flaws in Biff's life may change—in a few years. She will have to guard against mapping her personality, gifts, strengths, and expectations over Biff's capacities and demand he works through those things the way she has (1 Thessalonians 5:14). One of the worst mistakes a spouse can make is comparing her life with his life (2 Corinthians 10:12). You cannot mandate the things you've overcome in a lifetime or the things you don't struggle with on another person for emulation. We all battle differently.

We all grow and change individually—uniquely. Some people do change with courageous, compassionate, and competent care. Other folks never transform. Fallen people helping fallen people change can be a mess; it never goes how you hoped or planned. The key to helping a fallen person mature in Christ is addressing your fallenness first (Matthew 7:3-5, 18:35). If you neglect your weaknesses or sin patterns, you will become impatient with the other person who is not doing what you expect. This approach to soul care will disqualify you from cooperating with the Lord to produce righteousness in the person you long to see change.

Call to Action

I realize what I'm saying is challenging because I'm no different from you. I have people with whom I long to see change, which rarely happens as fast or to the degree I wish it did. The following questions have helped me calibrate my heart and guard my tongue as I think about cooperating with the Lord in their transformation. Perhaps you have an unchanging spouse or other loved one. Will you consider these questions? It would be great to share these things with a friend and work through the questions together.

1. Do you have genuine affection for your spouse? If not, you must begin here. It's not appropriate to correct someone with whom you do not have affection, even if the only affection you can muster up is that they are fellow image-bearers.
2. Can you set aside your desires while helping your spouse become a better person? Have you considered how the only way you can get your good desire is to die to it first, which you must if you want to work with God to restore your spouse in a spirit of gentleness (Galatians 6:1–2)?
3. How is the gospel affecting your heart regarding questions one and two? I'm thinking about how Christ set aside His preferences to redeem you. We must model the gospel at this point if we hope to see folks change.
4. Where is the best place to begin with your spouse, even though it's not the main thing you want him to change?
5. Is your encouragement of him more evident to him than your critique of him? If not, will you change this?
6. Who will walk with you as you spend the rest of your life discipling your husband?

3

Unique Couple

No book can help your unique husband to become a better husband like you can. Sure, there are a zillion books, and we have the Bible too. But when it comes to a wife's role in helping her husband mature in Christ, she is his most effective means of grace to transformation. A man's wife has a unique position to help a unique man grow into a unique representation of Jesus Christ. Of course, these ideas apply to a husband too. He should be cooperating with God while exegeting the Bible to bring customizable care to his wife, but for now, I want to talk about a wife's leadership opportunity in the marriage.

Supplemental Help

However, before my friends with an admirable sufficiency of Scripture worldview get up in arms about my remarks about the Bible, let me clarify. God's Word is sufficient for all matters regarding truth and godliness. We also have many practical books written by remarkable men and women to help us mature into Christlikeness. My point here is not to downplay those incredible tools but to speak to a different aspect of transformative grace—the unique wife of a unique man.

I have mentioned the word *unique* several times—on purpose—because that is what I want to bring to your attention. The Bible gives us guidelines, rules, principles, and much more to show us how we ought to live. What the Bible does not do is exegete the unique individual autobiographically. It can speak to eight billion people in specific and general transformative ways, but it will not get into the unique nook and crannies of a person's life.

After reading several books about their problems, a long list of individuals and couples have come to me seeking help with their problems. There was nothing wrong with their books. Their tension was similar to the Ethiopian eunuch reading from the Book of Isaiah, who needed someone to apply it uniquely to him (Acts 8:32). If we did not need each other, there would not be such a heavy emphasis on the "one another" passages in the New Testament.

Primary Help

Though I have a sufficiency of Scripture worldview, I don't believe in a kind of magic that says God's Word is all you need to iron all the wrinkles out of your life. You can speak honestly about the Bible without downgrading it. The Bible is the most incredible tool you could have to help a person change. But a Stradivarius sitting in the corner of the room is just that if nobody will pick it up to demonstrate what it can do.

The Bible is the Stradivarius; a husband needs a wife who can play one. The retort could be, "Why doesn't he do it himself?" That's fair. He should, but my aim is not as apparent as that. I want to elevate and envision a wife's value here, not talk as though she has no role, responsibility, or competency in complementing her husband (Genesis 2:18). I'm not speaking to her as though she is incompetent.

I know that the Bible is a transformative tool in a man's transformation toolbox, and he must step up and turn that wrench if he wants to be like Jesus. But he has more resources than God's Word and personal responsibility. His wife is in a unique position to come alongside him to help him to become the man of God that he should be (1 Timothy 3:16–17). Thus, I am speaking about her role, not what the Bible can or what he should do.

Unique Spouse

Every spouse comes from the dinged and dented section of the grocery store. Adam and Eve were the only two spouses that entered into a covenant in a perfect state. Of course, that relationship went to pot, and the rest of us came from their broken pots of clay (Romans 5:12; 2 Corinthians 4:7). The key for each spouse is to understand their unique brokenness rather than general brokenness and how their unique dysfunctions relate to each other.

Sadly, too many spouses do not consider the effects of their unique fallenness. They hit the honeymoon trail with high expectations of how their marriage will be. In six days, six weeks, or six months, reality bites, and it's at that point a spouse has to realign their thinking biblically rather than their preferred expectations. If they do not make this sanctification realignment, the disappointed spouse will compound the offending spouse's pre-existing problems—the ones the partner brought into the marriage.

Some of those disappointed spouses never come to terms with what I'm saying, and the mere mention of them complicating their spouse's pre-existing and ongoing condition tempts them to react harshly. I trust that the more rational mind understands this relational reality and realizes the biblical logic of what I'm saying. The process of this kind of marital breakdown happens in five steps:

1. All humans are flawed.
2. Two flawed individuals marry.
3. Each one brings unique flaws to the marriage.
4. Their marriage is now unique.
5. Each spouse should disciple the other uniquely.

Unique Story

Biff came from a dysfunctional childhood. His dad was an abuser. He learned the ropes early: to lay low and hope not to get verbally or physically hit. Biff's personality is also non-charismatic. Being passive is natural for him. After you add his dad's abuse to a pre-existing disposition to hang back, you get an introverted, shy, and insecure adult who struggles with the fear of man (Proverbs 29:25).

Biff entered into marriage with this unique childhood template—baggage, which became the foundation for his marriage and childrearing. He also brought into his covenant the habits of an insecure person, two of which were porn and anger. His porn use was an escape (relief) from the pressure of being backward, awkward, and shy. He was too scared to ask a girl on a date, so he took the easy way out through the false intimacy of solo sex, which brought perverted comfort and relief and an addiction that twisted his view of an intimate marital relationship.

His anger was his way of getting things done. He did not know how to have normal relationships, so he modeled his dad's method for acquiring what he wanted: anger (James 4:1-3). Anger is the insecure person's manipulative tactic to get something they want. Biff's porn and anger were two powerful, dominating, and perverted ways of thinking about relationships, which affected his wife and children.

Mable's Expectation

Mable came from the same dinged and dented section of the store, albeit a different shelf, but I won't get into her pre-marriage baggage. I will focus on the two options she has before her for discipling her husband, which is to accept or reject him. If she assumes her discipleship role, the first step is for Mable to transition from the dating season to the marriage season. They had periods where they were not together during dating, making it easier for them to be "on" when they were together.

Biff could pump up himself to create an image for Mable to fall in love with while they were together. Then he would deflate into his authentic self when Mable was not around. While dating, Mable could overlook whatever threads she saw dangling from Biff's garment. But once she "brought him home to stay," there was no hiding the real Biff. He was passive, lazy, self-focused, disinterested, insecure, and occasionally angry, with a secret addiction.

It would take a fantastic amount of grace, discernment, and wisdom for Mable to know the difference between dating a dysfunctional guy and marrying one. Her gospel call is to "set aside" what she wants today while partnering with God to rebuild a broken man for a better future. Too many spouses miss this opportunity, whether the husband or wife. It's like their wedding day had no past, sorrow, or dysfunction. It's Adamic amnesia.

Close the Gap

What we want in a spouse and what we get are always different. If a spouse does not have a rational view of the differences or a determination to work hard to close the gap, things will continually worsen. Post-honeymoon, the cold reality is for the brave and mature, not the unrealistic, idealistic, and needy. If Mable understands these things, she will see her husband as an empty love cup who uses her to feel better about himself—a sobering truth like a cold towel across the face.

Rather than being offended and reactive, she will get to work, asking God to help her cooperate with Him to restore Biff to the man he should be, the one he could not be because of past brokenness in the home. The blessedness of marriage is only comparable to the work you put into it. It does not sound fair, but sin never is. Biff is not hiding the ball any longer. Will Mable persevere? Will she be part of the Lord's restoration team (Galatians 6:1-2)?

Mable now knows she was dating Biff's representative, not the real person. Rather than being the victim, who vicariously takes on his sin, she chooses to beg God for an attitude of forgiveness while asking Him to provide the wisdom and practical strength she needs to help him turn around. God loves lavishing His empowering grace on humble hearts (James 4:6). Mable resists being the victim and is ready to dig in to help her husband walk out repentance practically.

Ready, Set, Go

There are many things for Mable to do, and as you already see, she is the best candidate to help Biff walk out repentance. How kind of the Lord to bring her into Biff's life to model and instruct him on what it means to be a Christian. Nobody has the insight or intimacy that Mable has with this unique man. She has the history, time, and opportunity. Biff's mentors will be helpful, too, albeit supplemental. Here are a few means to assist Mable with her unique man.

- Sunday morning messages will be excellent opportunities to reinforce what is happening at home.
- Prayer will be specific and detailed for Biff's change, and it will be comforting and refreshing for Mable.
- God's Word will guide her as she disciples him.
- Mable will have a mentor to guide her along—a Titus 2 lady.
- The sweet Holy Spirit will illuminate and empower her while convicting him.

With these means of grace, she is leading this discipleship opportunity in their marriage. In the next section, I will explain a few more practical thoughts for Mable. None of them will be like flipping a switch on or off. They are ideas that she must implement daily—for many years. Biff is a habituated man; he has patterns that have existed for decades, long before Mable met him. Mable will need to help him unlearn these things while teaching him how to change.

Practically Speaking

1. **Transition:** The first thing Mable can do is index forward from dating to marriage. It's two different seasons; the latter is what reveals who a person is. If she continues to live in a dating dream world, her disappointment will will overcome her.
2. **Accept:** As she transitions, she must accept the reality of her man's unique fallenness. He is who he is, which is not an excuse, but wishing him to be different will not make it happen. It's going to take work on her part.
3. **Put Off:** Mable will have to live in a daily state of putting off thoughts about expectations and preferences, which can form a stronghold in her mind. If that happens, she will complicate an already complex man.
4. **Partner:** The gospel is her reminder and call. She understands that she was an unlovely person once upon a time, and in her husband's case, he did not get the "gospel training" that she did. God wants her to partner with Him.
5. **Identify:** Mable wants to identify the issues, not so much the behaviors—though they are vital, but rather the underlying heart issues. The most significant one for Biff is the fear of man. As she cooperates with the Lord to help him untangle his deep-seated insecurity, it will allow him to

overcome his two primary behavior sins: addiction and anger.

6. **TWO MEANS:** Encouragement and strength are the two most effective tools to help Biff change.
   - **ENCOURAGEMENT:** The kindness of God (encouragement) leads to repentance. Biff only knows disapproval, rejection, and disparaging words. His problems will worsen if Mable is critical or outspoken in her disappointment with him; his problems will worsen. Part of how she encourages him is by overlooking a lot of sin. Mable will have to choose her words carefully. She will often need to keep her mouth shut; other times, she wants to uplift with edifying comments. Sometimes corrective care is essential.
   - **STRENGTH:** Mable's power will happen in two ways: one is self-control, and the other is not letting Biff run all over her. Self-control is God's power working through her, which is part of the fruit of the Spirit. There will be other times when Biff will try to manipulate her. She must stand up for herself, which she can do respectfully.

Call to Action

Biff's sanctification is not on Mable's shoulders. How he relates to God and others is on him, not the responsibility of others. Don't think of this as though what you do or don't do will be the cause of your spouse's actions. I hope you see this as an opportunity to cooperate with the Lord to restore a soul. Imagine finding a broken-down car in the junkyard and you get to work with a Master Mechanic to repair it. If spouses considered their partners this way, it would transform many marriages.

1. Are you married to a dysfunctional spouse? Of course, you are—next question.
2. Will you describe his unique brokenness? What happened to him? What were his shaping influences, including the decisions he has made?
3. Though you want to address his behaviors, you must consider their sources first. What drives him? Is it fear, a desire to control, shame, or self-reliance? Something else?
4. How are you cooperating with the Lord in restoring your spouse to Christlikeness?
5. How do you need to change so that you don't complicate his complications?

4

See No Problem

It is not unusual for a marriage to be out-of-balance or spiritually off-kilter. There are many reasons for this problem between two formerly inseparable people dating who now have something between them that keeps them asymmetrical. Before addressing how to deal with a spouse who does not see a problem in their marriage, I have a few ideas of how these partners could have been so in love at the beginning and drift apart within a few years. Afterward, I will provide a few practical solutions for the spouse who wants to restore the marriage.

Twenty-Two Bad Signs

The importance of this list is that the problem is rarely a spouse not seeing there is a problem, but there are hindrances or inhibitors that keep them from working on the marriage. Like the wife who says, "My husband does not talk," which is a lie. He does communicate, but he does not talk to her. When someone says, "My spouse does not see a problem in our marriage," they are probably missing the real issue. Something has caught them, keeping them from working on the marriage. Here are twenty-two possibilities.

1. They have differing affections for Christ.
2. One spouse is not a Christian.
3. One spouse becomes a Christian after marriage.

4. There are maturity disparities between them.
5. There are soul-capacity disparities.
6. They grow at a different spiritual pace.
7. They have different or competing sin patterns.
8. One partner lies about why they are growing apart.
9. One partner is in self-denial regarding their true self.
10. There are jealousy, envy, bitterness, or unforgiveness issues.
11. There is a lack of submission from the wife.
12. One spouse is clueless about how to be a spouse.
13. There is willful deception.
14. There is an intelligence disparity between them.
15. They came from different family settings.
16. They relate to people differently.
17. There are personality differences, e.g., outgoing, introverted.
18. A spouse is apathetic toward the marriage.
19. They are competitors.
20. They don't know how to disciple each other.
21. The husband has a "conquer and move on" mindset. (He has a wife; now he's off to other aspirations.)
22. They have competing personal preferences.

If your marriage is off-kilter, I'm sure several of these things contribute to the problems. The most significant and obvious matter is that they are on two different pages. Typically, one spouse is more in tune with what is going on and knows things have to change. The other spouse is in a sin pattern(s) that is now evident. As the patterns persist, the other spouse will insist on things changing, though transformation is not a guarantee.

If God Is Not First

Whatever the problems may be, the most critical issue is the spiritual dynamic: something is wrong between the husband, wife, and God. You can see how the first seven items have a spiritual component to them. Though everything listed relates to spirituality, #8-22 are manifestations, outcomes, or behaviors of the first seven. One through seven represents a person's authentic spirituality or how they relate to God. The difference between the two sections is between who a person is and what a person does. If God is actively working in a person's heart, the destructive behaviors in the marriage should autocorrect eventually.

For example, a spouse would be willing to set aside their preferences (#22) if they had a profound and growing affection for Christ (#1). If they do not have a deep and growing love for Christ, marital disunity will continue. This perspective is one of the things that is so troubling about people getting married. The couple gives a courtesy nod to spiritual affections while elevating other stuff like (1) compatibility, (2) preferences, (3) family background, (4) appearance, (5) finances, and (6) whether they "go to church" or not. While all of these have their ranking in the "who I want to marry" lineup, none of them are more critical than an individual's spiritual affections.

Many pastors and counselors are more interested in testing the aspiring couple for compatibility than discerning the couple spiritually. Before there were psychological evaluations, there was spiritual discernment. It does not take much to know if a person is a good fit for marriage. Sadly, spiritual affections get pushed to the side. After five years (or less), they begin drifting apart. If they have children within this timeframe, they can chug along because of the distractions and pace of being a family. Perhaps they limp to the empty nest stage before their ongoing problems intensify.

Marry a God-lover

If a spouse has a strong, deep, and growing affection for God, there is a good chance the person they choose will want to be like them (1 Corinthians 11:1). Christ had deep affections for His Father, which positioned Him to help others mature as Christ-followers. Notice the formula: his affection for the Father impacted those around Him (John 6:38). Imagine if a boyfriend or husband had a fixation on doing the will of God. Wow! This kind of spiritual attitude would enable him to overcome any marital challenge. Go back to the six things that some lovers look for in a marriage partner. Apply them to Christ. They all would fall woefully short.

- **COMPATIBILITY:** He was not compatible with us.
- Preferences: He had distinctly different preferences from us.
- **FAMILY BACKGROUND:** His "family background" was other-worldly.
- **APPEARANCE:** He was not much to look at—not the "sexiest" pick in Israel by a long shot (Isaiah 53:2).
- **FINANCES:** His pillow was a rock, and His ceiling was the sky. He wasn't financially loaded while living with us.
- **CHURCH:** He didn't go to church. He was the church.

Jesus had one thing that made Him a great catch. He loved His Father with all His heart, soul, mind, and strength. If you're not happily married, you may react with, "Well, thanks, Rick. That's great. I see it now, but I've made my bed, and it's pretty darn uncomfortable to sleep in when considering who is sleeping beside me. What do I do now?" I'm not saying these things to rub your nose in an immature or unwise decision, but if I can break up immoral or unwise dating relationships, what I've said is well-worth hearing.

Gospel Beginnings

But what about you? You married a person who does not have deep and growing spiritual affections. What do you do? What can you do? The first thing to consider is what I've said about spiritual affections. Your spouse must change their relationship with God before focusing on marriage issues. If you are growing apart, the biggest problem is your spouse's understanding and application of the gospel.

The gospel is about God reconciling humanity to Himself. It's about unity, healing, redemption, adopting, justifying, sanctifying, and glorifying. These are some of the things that the gospel does. If you and your spouse are growing apart or managing the status quo, the gospel has lost its power in your relationship. The gospel is where you must begin. Your marriage is not something you can fix through your strength or a self-help marriage book. The gospel is not something to purchase, manipulate, bargain with, or control. It is a work of grace—free gift—in a person's life.

We came to know the gospel because of God's free grace, which empowered us to change. May I remind you again? Rarely does someone need a "new truth." What they need is an old truth. They need reminding of what they already know. They need to hear the gospel again. Carefully read this passage, and as you do, think about what you already know about the gospel. Consider how free it was and how you could not make it happen. God, according to His mysterious mercy, made it happen to you.

> But God, being rich in mercy, because of the great love with which he loved us, even when we were dead in our trespasses, made us alive together with Christ—*by grace you have been saved*—and raised us up with him and seated us with him in the heavenly

places in Christ Jesus, so that in the coming ages he might show the immeasurable riches of his grace in kindness toward us in Christ Jesus. For by grace, you have been saved through faith. And this is not your own doing; it is the gift of God, not a result of works, so that no one may boast.
(Ephesians 2:4-9)

Prayer Works

You probably already discerned the first place you have to go regarding your spouse and their lack of spiritual connectivity. It's to your knees. If you want your spouse to love you the right way, you have to go to the Father on their behalf. A person cannot love anyone correctly, effectively, or sufficiently until they love God most of all. Our hearts (#1-7) and behaviors (#8-22) must not be out-of-sync. If our hearts and actions mirror each other, we will learn how to love each other correctly. No person can love God with all his heart, soul, mind, and strength and not love his spouse and others wonderfully well.

- How often and to what degree do you pray for your spouse?
- What is the content of your prayers?
- How are you soliciting others to pray with you?

The best and the most helpful thing you can do is spend time before your heavenly Father, on behalf of your spouse, pleading for His mercy to be let loose for His glory and mutual benefit. Once you properly align your heart with the Lord and actively seek Him on behalf of your spouse, you want to spend time assessing yourself. A few good friends are vital at this point.

Sober Assessment

Few things are more potent than a transforming life. If the gospel transforms you, it will give your spouse fewer reasons to fuss. If you talk to your spouse about assessing you, prepare for an inappropriate response. If you ask how you can change or serve your spouse more effectively, they may tell you unkindly, and you may not hear the truth wrapped up by their unkindness. (If your spouse is a fool, who is unwilling to have a civil conversation with you, I do not recommend talking with them. That kind of marriage is beyond the scope of some of the ideas I'm sharing with you.)

Let's say your spouse is 75 percent off in their assessment. Did you hear the 25 percent of truth within the unkindness? It takes a spiritual person to listen to the truth when the message is harsh or partly inaccurate, but if you're more interested in God's glory than your feelings, you will be okay. God will give you grace, and you can change. Christ had to ignore a lot of our nonsense to honor His Father. We were the knuckleheads who regularly messed things up, but His focus was not on His felt needs.

He kept His eye on the ball. Perhaps the Spirit of God wants to address something in your life. Maybe He will use a knucklehead to bring it to light. Listen to what the Spirit wants you to hear and make those changes. What you don't want to do is get in the way of God's work. If there are two problems on the table, start by taking one of them off the table. Though God can efficiently multitask by working on both of you simultaneously, why not cooperate with Him by keeping in step with the Spirit and making the changes you need to make?

Prepare for the Worst

May the Lord devote His total effort to your spouse. Be the Father's cooperative servant. It could be that your spouse will not change or maybe not change according to your timetable. I do not understand why it would be that way, but I do know it can be, and it has been for many spouses. This possibility is where you will have to check your heart. A few close friends can serve you here. God is not obligated to tell you His plans or give you what you want the way you want it. He has called you to do one thing: trust Him.

Your marriage is an act of faith. You never know what you're going to get from it. But there is one thing that you can find rest and assurance in, and it's this: God loves you, and He is working for your good (Romans 8:28). There have been many times when it was hard to believe what I just typed. You must often remind yourself of this message, especially if your spouse does not change. Regardless of the outcome, you will stand in heaven and praise God for every decision the Lord made and how He led you all the way.

My former wife left me in 1988 for another man and took our two children with her. It was the worst possible nightmare. If you have lost your children, you understand. If you have children, you feel the pain in your soul as you think about losing them. Never in a million years would I want to repeat those ten years, but I would not change them for anything—at this point. In that crucible of unrelenting suffering, I found God—many years after He regenerated me. While I often sinned during those days, God never left me. He always persevered with me. God was stunning. He has never changed.

Praise Is Coming

I look back on those days and praise God for the journey. Sometimes I praise Him through tears because sin leaves marks. Perhaps you can't praise God today, and you don't think you ever will. Let's be honest: if you know Him, you will praise Him someday. You know God is with you, and He will not leave you. He is working His best in your life. Your issues are more about:

1. Accepting the current reality of the situation
2. Setting aside what you prefer for a greater good
3. Cooperating with God in His work in your life
4. Hoping for a better day, which will come
5. Actively trusting God through the process

Those five things can converge in your mind and put you in a spiritual funk if you allow them. Still yet, God is with you. Though you may not be able to persevere with God, He will persevere with you. He is there, and He will bring you through this situation. Someday you will see and know these things to be true, and your affections for God will be more intense than they are now.

Call to Action

1. Work through the list of twenty-two items. Divide the spiritual heart issues from the behaviors. Which ones from each category belong to you? Which ones belong to your spouse?
2. What is your specific and detailed plan to change yourself? Who will you enlist to help you change?
3. What is the correlation between your spouse's spiritual issues and the behaviors? I'm asking, how do the spiritual issues influence the behaviors?
4. Write several prayers for your spouse that relate to your analysis of the list. Appeal to God daily to work in your spouse's heart.
5. Keep a journal of positive changes you see in your spouse. Thank God for this progress and continue to pray for more transformation.
6. What does it mean to be in a crucible of suffering? How is God using the suffering of your marriage to mature you?
7. How are your preferences, desires, wants, and wishes hindering the growth that could be happening in your life? How could they hinder the work of God in your spouse's life? What is your practical and specific plan to change? Who is going to help you through this process?

5

An Imperfect Person

Imperfect people are a universal problem. Most of the time, we do not struggle with the quirks of our fallenness—until we start living with one of those imperfect people. When you put two sinners in a box for an extended period, there will be problems, making it essential to have a game plan for living with an imperfect person. I have seven tips for your consideration as I weave the life and times of three quirky people I know into this all-important discussion about individuals and those things that can get under our skin.

Quirky People

Biff and Mable came to our home. Upon entering, and while I wasn't looking, Biff turned one of our lampshades cockeyed. Biff knew I would eventually notice and readjust the crooked shade. A few moments later, I was talking to Biff and noticed the lampshade over his right shoulder. I excused myself and went to straighten it. I resumed our conversation. Biff laughed. I asked him why he was laughing, and he said he tilted the shade on purpose. We both laughed because I do notice things. I have always observed stuff. It's who I am. God made me observant, literal, and detailed—a blessing and a curse.

The curse part is that sometimes I can get on my friends' nerves, though my closest friends are humble, making my little quirk a non-issue. Biff and others have enjoyed making fun of me through the years. We all have our quirks. Our son is like me. He has quirks. I recall asking him to go upstairs and retrieve something from our bedroom. He bounded up the stairs, and by the time he got to the upper landing, he had forgotten why he was there. That is our son. He is absolutely adorable, honest, and sincere and seems to find no greater joy than serving people. But he can be absent-minded. His focus needs sharpening. I love him dearly and believe he will make a special lady happy someday. But he tends to lose his sense of awareness from time to time. It is not intentional. It is part of his personality.

Then there is my adorable wife. It is well-known within our small circle of friends that she "cannot tell time." I say she lives on "island time." There is a reason we call her "Saint Lucia." We also labeled her "The Rocket." It is our way of poking fun at her. If she goes into a store to buy one item, it could take thirty minutes. Though she is near "omnicompetent" and could run a small country, she also loses focus regarding time management. In all three of these illustrations, there are no sin issues involved. Our son does not willfully forget things so that he can irritate me. My wife is not premeditating about how she can tempt me by losing track of time. I do not measure and straighten every item in our home to see whom I can annoy.

No Clones

We all have at least one thread hanging out of our garments that reminds us of our imperfections. Can we adjust a few of our personality peculiarities? Of course, we can. Anyone can change some things, and we can always pray about our quirks. We can ask God to help us change where and when appropriate. We can encourage and assist each other too, but at some point, we must understand how our personalities will be what they are. There is always a unique way about our fallenness, but we must distinguish between different personalities and sin.

We must not condone wrong thinking and behaviors, but we should embrace and leverage our uniqueness. We get into trouble regarding personality differences when we try to change people to be like us. For example, I could arrogantly believe what comes naturally to me should be easy for everyone. Why can't my family walk into any living room and notice which lampshades are 16mm off? You'd have to be pretty ignorant not to see what I see. Of course, you respond by saying you have better things to do than keeping track of lampshade tilts. I would say you are right.

One of the most natural sins to commit is when we impose our view of how secondary issues ought to be for everyone. Our differences should bring glory to God while benefiting each other. When I first married Lucia, I thought we could do more if she were like me. Later, I saw the foolishness of that thinking. I praise God that my wife is not like me. God made her a particular way, and it has been His kindness to help me see and appreciate those differences. I now understand how difficult our life would have been if she were a "Ricky clone."

Imperfect People

I trust these helpful pointers will serve you as you grow in your relationships with imperfect people. These thoughts are a collaborative work that Lucia and I came up with and, by the grace of God, try to model in our home.

#1 Release Imperfect Friends: God made your friends a certain way. Part of every Christian's job is to help each other mature into the unique vessels God is shaping them to be. To pick on, degrade, criticize, condemn, or discourage your friend will impede the grace of God in them and your relationship. If you are harsh or unkind, your friend will never be able to realize all that God has prepared for them to be. There is a unique relationship between a couple or parents and children or Christian friends. Christians are part of the body of Christ. The Lord forms Christ in our spouses, children, and friends. Our job is to cooperate with God by serving our friends in their ongoing progressive sanctification. John Donne said in Meditation 17, "No man is an island of itself; every man is a piece of the continent, a part of the main."

1. How are you releasing the imperfect people in your life to realize and experience what God is shaping in them?
2. Do you make them more concerned about your opinion of them or God's opinion of them?
3. Are your friends free to be themselves when you are not around, or are they more guarded around you?

#2 DON'T BE SURPRISED: Having a full view of the doctrine of sin is essential when building relationally with others. If you don't, you will be surprised when they sin. You should never be surprised when a person sins. Sinning is one of the things we are good at doing. The most apparent implication of the gospel is that people sin, which is why Christ died. Remember? If we did not sin, all the planning and orchestrating by God to bring His Son to earth to die on a Roman cross for sinners would be lunacy. He died for sinners. Sinners will sin. If our first instinct is to get mad, upset, frustrated, disappointed, and critical when a person sins, we have not made it to first base in our understanding of the gospel or our relationships. My point here is dealing with sin, though the point of the chapter is about non-sin-related issues. I'm primarily writing about how different personalities can tempt us to sin, not how actual sins affect us. It is essential to understand how wrong responses to sin and quirks aren't helpful in relationship building.

1. How do you respond when imperfect people sin? Do you expect imperfect people to be perfect all of the time?
2. Are you more focused on what they do wrong or how you can help them become like Christ?
3. Will you talk with them about your perspective of them and how it affects you?

#3 Be an Encourager: If you are more apt to get bent out of shape when a person does not do something the way you think they ought to, you will likely create a culture of fear in your relationships. Once that culture develops, it will be tough to make it right. It will make folks guarded, insecure, and second-guess themselves. They will decrease, and you will increase (John 3:30). If you have a critical spirit, you will exasperate your friends. It is not a good relationship whenever a person breathes a sigh of relief when you are gone. I had a relationship like this. Whenever I was around him, it was like being "Muhammed Ali's verbal punching bag." It was a good day if my day did not include him. I had to psyche myself up just being around him. In time, I became a completely different person. While I'm not putting all of the dysfunction of the relationship solely in this person's lap, I have felt released from prison since the relationship dissolved. My heart aches for many people, especially spouses, who cannot biblically walk away as I did from what must feel like a life sentence.

1. Are you an encourager? Is this how others would characterize you?
2. Do your friends mature as they are affected by your relationship with Christ?

3. Do you seek to shape your friends into another version of you or Jesus? Does God become more prominent in their eyes after they spend time with you, or do you become more significant in their eyes?

#4 Discern the Situation: Few things in our marriage have been worth arguing about. Though neither of us has kept a record of wrongs, we agree that most of our disagreements have been over preferences. Rarely do we argue over things God would deem important enough to discuss at that level of intensity. When my wife is late or makes me late, I am more concerned with my reputation than whatever she may be doing. If our kids were not making a suitable grade or performing according to my preferences, the temptation is to think more about how it reflects on me. If I am not careful and regularly repenting, it becomes how others perceive me than what is vital to God. I can quickly lose track of God's perspective as my discernment meter shuts down because I have made a mountain out of a molehill.

1. How many crucial things have you fought over recently with your spouse? How often do you view the situation from God's perspective versus yours?
2. How often does your reputation interfere with how you discern the situation?
3. Are you being intellectually honest when you hold firm to your convictions? Are they convictions?

#5 Be Humble and Confess: We all have sinned when responding to others. The only way we can fix our improper responses to our imperfect friends is by humbly confessing those sins and seeking forgiveness from the ones we have hurt. If we do not own our sins, there is no possible way to rectify the situation. The hard part is how our unwillingness to own our sins speaks to our most potent and core sin issues: self-righteousness and self-sufficiency. The self-righteous person has a greater-than attitude that exalts oneself over others. They are relying on themselves rather than trusting God. Whenever I sin to justify my actions, my argument has holes. If I continue to press my case, I will dig a deeper hole, and the people I am trying to convince will relationally distance themselves from me.

1. Are you quick to confess your sins? What is the most common theme in your life: confession to others or correcting others?
2. Which of the two does your spouse receive the most from you—your confession or correction?
3. If you correct more than confess, would you be willing to dismantle your self-sufficiency and find help? Write your repentance plan and share it with your spouse or a close friend.

#6 LIVE WITHIN THE COMMUNITY: I had a friend who tried to get rid of a particular sin issue, and after he experienced a season of success, he would confess it to his wife. He lived a cyclic life, and his marriage rode the roller coaster with him. I appealed to him for nearly a year to share his struggle with his wife. He did. They are on the road to mending the brokenness in their marriage. He is doing this in a community. I'm well aware most of the people who interact with our ministry do not have the kind of community that can serve them in their struggles. One of the reasons our ministry exists is because of a breakdown in some local churches. Also, it is not unusual for a person to come to me asking that their church not know anything about their situation. I will honor their request most of the time, though it saddens me how the relationship between them and their local body is divisive and secretive. A healthy body has a healthy immune system, analogous to the body of Christ. Paul wrote mostly for local churches.

He urged church people to do effective "one another-ing."

1. Do you belong to a small group of friends? Do your friends really, really know you?
2. Do they know things about you, but you withhold the real you from them?
3. Will you trust God with your life by being more humble and revealing to those who love you?

#7 REMEMBER THE GOSPEL: Some people say, "Rick, you are Johnny One-Note." I guess I unashamedly am. The gospel not only defines my starting point, but it sets my trajectory, as well as my ending point. For me, all of life is about the gospel. If our life is not about the gospel, it is a waste, and we will tragically miss its point. While there are many implications of the gospel, there is one significant implication we need to gain from this chapter: I am a bigger sinner than any person I know. If this truth rivets your soul, it will radically alter your relationships.

1. Do you spend more time speck fishing than examining the log in your eye? (Matthew 7:3–5).
2. Who is the most prominent sinner in your life? (1 Timothy 1:15).
3. What is the main point of your relationships: to serve or for others to serve you? (Mark 10:45).

Call to Action

Will you walk through all the questions in this chapter with a close friend, preferably your spouse? Adding your children and friends to this discussion would benefit you immensely.

6

How to Be Honest

How honest can you be with your spouse? Is your marriage vulnerable, safe, and robust enough to communicate honestly? Are you free from critique and condemnation, releasing you to talk transparently with your mate? How much have things changed since dating, when communication was not as cumbersome, constricted, or convoluted? Perhaps speaking freely in your marriage has become more challenging as the years go by, and if that is the case, I trust what I have to say will be the beginning of a new day.

Start with God

When thinking about these questions, it would be best to begin by focusing on how you relate to the Lord. Whatever happens in our relationships on earth, we should not disconnect them from how we relate to our heavenly Father. For example, God calls us to imitate Him (Ephesians 5:1). What better way to do that than in our relationships? Thus, we think about relating to others by reflecting on how we think about and relate to God, providing us with a template for interacting with humans. Where would you want your starting point for communication to begin—with you, your spouse, or the Lord? Let's start with God because I suspect you are open, honest, and transparent with Him. You freely talk to Him (prayer), and He freely speaks to you (Bible).

> *For he himself is our peace, who has made us both one and has broken down in his flesh the dividing wall of hostility.*
>
> (Ephesians 2:14)

Although your relationship with God is not perfect because you're not perfect, you are maturing in your relationship with Him, forming the foundation for how you relate to others. Your heavenly Father teaches you how to engage others, even if those relationships are complicated. Perhaps recalling your hostile relationship with God before He regenerated you will reset the stage for talking to others (Ephesians 2:1-10). God is the hostility remover who enables us to enjoy peace with Him and others. We export what He has freely given to us. But you may say, "Rick, you're crazy. That's impossible! You don't know my spouse." I agree with you on all points. I'm probably a little crazy. It is impossible—at least impossible, apart from the grace of God, and I do not know your spouse.

What I do know is what a Christian marriage could be like and how we should strive to imitate the life of Christ in our marriages (1 Corinthians 11:1). Imitating Jesus and exporting His life and values to others is what all Christians should be doing. Think briefly about what it could look like if you chose to imitate God in your marriage. You can do this by considering two ways you relate to the Lord. There are many ways to emulate Him, but I want to focus on two for this chapter. The first is that He does not condemn us. Therefore, we should strive to live in a non-condemning marriage. The second is that He wants to listen to us. Therefore, we should be quick to listen to our spouses.

No Condemnation

There is therefore now no condemnation for those who are in Christ Jesus.

(Romans 8:1)

God never condemns, mocks, criticizes, or puts us down when we share our hearts with Him (Ephesians 4:29). He is always ready to listen and is prepared to help. The Lord knows our frames and understands our weaknesses. He desires to uplift, encourage, and speak into our situations with love (Psalm 103:12–14). I'm sure you appreciate this characteristic of the Lord, but how does it work out in your marriage? Have you ever put something out there for your spouse to hear only to quickly retract it because your moment of transparency collided with unkindness or disinterest?

Mable has longed for an open and honest relationship with her husband, Biff. She has ventured into the transparent zone with him through the years only to meet criticism and mocking. When she tried to be transparent, she felt his critique most of the time. It would sting, which motivated her to withdraw. Little by little, the distance between them became greater and greater. Biff was clueless about these communication flaws in their relationship. From his perspective, everything was okay because they were not fighting. When they did fight, he typically rebuked her by letting her know where she was wrong. If he messed up and could not wiggle out of his actions, he would do a quick flyover to smooth things out, which was his way of justifying his actions. Then he would be off to the next thing.

Mable found more community in her ladies' Bible study on Tuesday mornings than with Biff. She felt unheard, misunderstood, and immature for mentioning her little annoyances about him (1 Peter 3:7). Their marriage problems created pockets of silence in her heart, where she insulated herself from Biff's insensitivity. He did not know this when I brought it up during a counseling session. It soon became apparent that he knew little about Mable's secret life. She was lonely on the inside, a dangerous place for any woman longing for a relationship. Though she did not discern it initially, she began to drift from her relationship with Biff (and from the Lord). Social media, texting, and Bible study were her primary communication substitutes. She was aware of the growing bitterness in her heart, but she felt trapped in her marriage.

Though she had resigned herself to "this is the way it will always be," she did not like how things were. She was not only vulnerable to the alluring temptations of social media, texting, and her Bible study, but she was unwittingly open to any caring male relationship. Mable and Biff had drifted from the goal of being open and honest with each other. It was worse than that. They were heading in opposite directions. After the children leave the house and Biff retires, it will be difficult for them to stay married. Unless Biff finds a hobby and Mable continues her social media fascination, being together will be one long silence until death gives Mable the freedom she desires. As you think through any condemnation aspects of your marriage, these questions can apply to either gender.

Time to Reflect

- When your spouse shares their heart with you, is your posture inviting and desirous to learn more?
- Are you quick to answer, or are you ready to listen while asking clarifying questions so you can understand (James 1:19)?
- How often do you ask your spouse about their "secret thoughts?" Do you seek to explore them with your spouse?
- Do you see your spouse as an inexhaustible discovery to enjoy or as an exhausting human being?

- Do your spouse's weaknesses get on your nerves? How are you discipling your spouse through those imperfections?

Ready to Listen

Do nothing from rivalry or conceit, but in humility count others more significant than yourselves.
(Philippians 2:3)

This second aspect of imitating Jesus in your marriage focuses on Christ's lack of self-interest. One of the statements I like about the gospel is that if it anchors you, there is nothing to fear, defend, lose, or hide. Jesus is like that. He is so secure in His relationship with me that He can take my angry responses and other ways I express my disappointment to Him. We are allowed to let Him know what we're thinking. Jesus is about us. He dramatically proved this by going to the cross in our place. Though we should never be angry with God, it is possible, and if that were the case, our anger would never disorient Him. He would listen to and love us in response (Romans 5:8; 1 John 4:8). That is the kind of love husbands and wives should imitate and enjoy.

> *I still have many things to say to you, but you cannot bear them now.*
> *(John 16:12)*

Biff is immature and insecure. If Mable says anything related to him, their marriage, and the need for change, Biff takes it personally and usually sulks in response to her remarks. Mable does not believe she can be candid with him because of his insecurities. This issue causes her to take a guarded posture around Biff. Rather than speaking openly and honestly about what is going on with them, it is more like talking to a child, where she must measure every word, weighing them before she can share them. She is pulling double duty: not only does she have to care for her soul, but she also has to care for her husband. She has to grow him up before he can contribute to their mutual marital sanctification. She tries not to be self-righteous about it, but it is hard. Biff is a weak, immature, and insecure husband.

He does not process things through a scriptural lens. He interprets stuff through his past personal experiences and hurts. His dad was a mean and condemning man who had a significant adverse shaping influence on Biff's life. Whenever anyone says anything negative to Biff, he becomes defensive and argumentative and feels the need to justify himself or retaliate. These reactions make Biff a tedious man, which weighs heavy on Mable's soul. She grows weary of being around him because of his deep fear-of-man problems. There is ongoing and seemingly unresolvable inequitable-ness in their relationship. It is similar to a college student married to an eighth grader. Biff is so different from Christ. He esteems himself more than his wife, which disables him from being Christ to her.

Time to Reflect

- Are you mature enough to listen to your spouse without feeling threatened? If not, how do you need to change? What is your plan to change?
- Will you filter what your spouse says through the lens of Scripture rather than your personal experience? What does it mean to do this? Will you spend time wrestling with God and seeking a competent friend to teach you?
- Will you embrace and engage your spouse's words from a position of God's strength rather than through your weaknesses? Understanding self-reliance versus

God-reliance is essential. You must know these differences and learn to rely on God rather than yourself.
- Will you listen to your spouse when they share hurts, or are you more concerned with how their words affect you? If this is a problem in your marriage, will you confess this to your spouse and begin the change process?
- Which is more important: to be more right than your spouse or to serve your spouse? What does your response reveal about your relationship with God?

Call to Action

As you think about this chapter and how it applies to your spouse, whether your husband or wife needs to change, here are three tips to factor into your thoughts about the question sets I've presented.

Tip #1: Presence, Not Perfection: When a couple becomes married, they will not have perfected their communication. After twenty years of marriage, they will not have perfect communication. I appeal to these couples not to get hung up on or expect perfection in how their spouse talks. As you think about your marriage, give less consideration to the ideal of a virtue and more time to cultivate its presence. For example, I am not asking if you have perfected the gift of encouragement, but will you encourage others at all? Do you have an encouragement gene? If you are more about condemning and critiquing, the place to begin is to ask the Lord to teach you how to encourage.

Tip #2: Determine the Direction: Are you both pointed in the right direction? Are you seeking daily to remove the outer layer of fig leaves so you can grow closer together (Genesis 3:7)? If you are not heading in the right direction, I appeal to you to change your course. You must repent. You do not have to go through your marriage problems alone. They may not change, but you can surround yourself with a loving, caring, and competent community to hold you accountable while experiencing encouragement in the journey.

Tip #3: Resist Self-righteousness: The quickest of all traps is to take on the victim mindset, elevating yourself above your mate. Typically, the victim will have a sanctified morality that blinds them to their self-righteousness and harsh responses to their spouse. (I'm not speaking of physically harmful marriages, but regular run-of-the-mill marriage problems.) It's essential that the spouse struggling with an unchanging mate insists their friends be honest with how they perceive them. The hurting spouse must be open to their friends' courageous and compassionate correctives, or they will fall into the victim trap, sanitizing their anger responses and complicating the already struggling marriage.

Finally, I mentioned two ways we can imitate the Lord in our marriages: no condemnation and listening well.

1. What other communicable attributes of God can you imitate in your marriage to make it more Christlike?
2. Will you discuss these things with your spouse and make these talks part of your times of reflection together until they become Christocentric habituations?
3. If you're unable to have these talks with your spouse, will you find that competent, courageous, and compassionate friend to walk with you for a season?

7

Setting Aside

A wife can be a husband's most significant asset or his greatest liability. Most of us know this because people who live with each other affect those in the home—for good or evil. However, I wonder how many wives have thought through how much of an asset they are to their husbands by coming alongside them to complement, advise, share their wisdom, and disciple him, even while being submitted to them. The dual role of participating in the husband-and-wife hierarchy while living as a coequal is of inestimable value to any marriage.

Equal in Marriage

WARNING: If your spouse is physically harming you, my strongest appeal is for you to speak with a competent biblical leader before you act on what I'm teaching. If your husband manipulates you, please talk to someone. I'm writing to marriages with normal problems, not hyperbolic issues where one spouse may harm the other.

Though the Lord calls the wife to a unique role of submission in the marriage, it does not mean she has no leadership capabilities and should not use those strengths to bless her husband. With this in mind, may I ask you a couple of questions about how you humbly lead your husband by the example you model in your home? How are you using your gifts, strengths, skills, and talents to help your husband be a better leader? How do you use your God-given insight and wisdom to guide and mature your husband? I have often asked these questions to wives, and they do not always respond the same way. Here are three typical responses.

- The Humble Response: "I didn't know I could help him lead. Tell me more."
- The Angry Response: "Why does he need me to help him do what he should do?"
- The Victim Response: "Why are you putting the weight of his failures in my lap?"

Let me tackle the third response first. If he has failures, they are between him and God and are not your fault. We have a moral responsibility before God not to sin, and it's unacceptable to blame others for what God expects us to do (James 4:17). The point of my questions comes from a "brother's keeper perspective," not an accusatory one. My questions were not about your being culpable regarding what he is doing wrong, but about you living out the gospel in practical and specific ways before God and your husband. Though Christ was not responsible for our sins, He deliberately came alongside us to help us while we were failing miserably.

> But God shows his love for us in that while we were still sinners, Christ died for us.
> (Romans 5:8)

See the Need

Jesus was not at fault for what we did wrong, but He saw a need and found great joy in helping us to overcome our problems (Hebrews 12:1–2). Christ realized that our condition was more significant than our ability to fix it, so

He humbled Himself to death on the cross. I'm not asking you to do what He did in a literal sense, but we must be willing to take up our unique crosses for the sake of others, especially our spouses. You may even recall the story in the Bible about the good Samaritan that communicates this idea of recognizing a problem and doing what is within our power and scope to assist.

> But a Samaritan, as he journeyed, came to where he was, and when he saw him, he had compassion. He went to him and bound up his wounds, pouring on oil and wine. Then he set him on his own animal and brought him to an inn and took care of him. Which of these three, do you think, proved to be a neighbor to the man who fell among the robbers? He said, "The one who showed him mercy." And Jesus said to him, "You go, and do likewise."
> (Luke 10:33-34, 37)

The point of this story is when we see a need, we should seek to respond to that need if we can. This man saw a need and decided to set aside his plans for the day to help a fellow struggler. One of the more profound demonstrations of the gospel in a marriage is when a wife is willing to set aside what she wants because of a greater desire to serve her husband so he can become a better leader in the marriage, home, and community. This kind of others-centered attitude is at the heart of the gospel (Philippians 2:5-11).

Follow Jesus

> Do nothing from selfish ambition or conceit but in humility count others more significant than yourselves.
> (Philippians 2:3)

The Father is appealing to us to set aside our preferences for the greater good of others. The good news is that dying to ourselves to come alongside a fellow struggler is not the end of the story. Jesus died to help us. In time, He will thoroughly enjoy the fruit of His sacrifice with millions of people who have accepted the gospel. It can be easy for a wife to lose this Christocentric gospel focus because of the difficulties and demands of being a wife to an exasperating man. The dawning awareness of how the husband is not what she hoped he would be can be disappointing, frustrating, and overwhelming.

Perhaps she spent most of her young life waiting for her prince to come. Then he showed up. She married him—only to be surprised at the revelation of what she did not know during the dating season, which came shortly after the honeymoon. Her hope for a good marriage had more control over her than God's call to model a Christlike example to a challenging person. Who has not had this experience? Instead of working toward maturing the marriage through her humility, wisdom, strengths, and practical help, her dashed hopes overpowered her and interfered with what God could have done through her. She became entangled by what she wanted versus what God could do. She responded with anger toward him.

Be Jesus

The standard retort when I make these appeals typically run along the line of, "You don't know my husband." Of course, that would be correct; I don't know anyone's husband the way their wives do; I don't live with him. But I am assuming that he is like me, and if, perchance, he is like me, his temptations are generally selfish. Sometimes he succumbs to those unsavory temptations, causing insensitivity and stubbornness—if he is like me. I do not know your husband, but perhaps leveling the playing field would be helpful. Do you sin in response to some of your husband's behaviors? If you do, this is where you need to begin leading him. Nobody can righteously make a case for sinning against someone, regardless of what they have done to them.

If you have sinned against your husband because of his sin or general thick-headedness, you have found the right place to begin leading him. You can do this through humble confession of your sin and seeking his forgiveness. How wonderful could that be for him? If he needs to repent, lead him by your example of repentance. Isn't this how we parent our children? You teach your children through your example, knowing a picture is worth a thousand words. Imagine what a clear representation of the humble Christ would look like to a person who desperately needs to see Jesus in somebody's life.

The temptation is to focus more on what our marriages are not giving us rather than regularly providing what our marriages need, which is our Christlike examples. Do you know how to serve your husband this way? God has repeatedly used my wife's strengths throughout our marriage to help me be a better husband and leader. She has been a remarkable practical example of Christ's actions in Philippians chapter two. Lucia has, on many occasions, set aside her preferences to quietly and courageously lead me to a greater understanding of Christ. Her posture has convicted me of sin while motivating me to be a better leader in our home.

Examining Motives

Another response is, "What if I do all this and my husband does not change?" It's a possibility, but that should not be the first question we should ask. The first thought should be, "Why am I doing this for our marriage? What is my motive?" Do you model Christ before your husband primarily because you want him to change, or do you model Christ because you want to honor God regardless of what your husband does? There is a possibility that your husband will never change. It happens. A story in the Bible is about a young rich man who would not change. When he encountered the Savior, Jesus asked him to sell all he had and follow Christ. "But when he heard these things, he became very sad, for he was extremely rich" (Luke 18:23).

I do not know what happened to this man. The Bible does not tell us. We do know what happened to Jesus. He kept being Jesus even when others around Him would not emulate His example. God gives grace to the humble (James 4:6), and if you walk in the humility of Christ (1 Peter 2:20-25), even when you are not getting all you want, you will be repeatedly surprised by His grace. I wish I could tell you something different, but I can't. I talk to people weekly who want better marriages, children, parents, or a better life. Sometimes it does not work out the way they want. That is the reality of the fallen world in which we live.

But there are some things that we can do, even when others will not cooperate with our desires. I had a friend give me a piece of advice in 1989, and I have never forgotten it. He said, "I can't make you love me, but you can't stop me from loving you." He shared this during a season when I desperately wanted my wife to change her mind about our relationship. She never changed her mind, and I fully felt the helplessness of our unchangeable situation. My friend's advice became invaluable, and I have used it many times since. I never got what I wanted and had to learn not to let that disappointment manage me. I have since thought about his advice this way:

> God so loved the world that He was bound and determined to lavish the world with His Son even if the world did not reciprocate. His love was so profound that He gave His one and only Son to save a bunch of unlovable people. And by doing this, He

left the door open for anyone to accept His love. If they did respond to His grace, great. If they did not, their rejection would not alter His love for them.

(John 3:16 paraphrase)

What's Your Motive?

And no creature is hidden from his sight, but all are naked and exposed to the eyes of him to whom we must give account.

(Hebrews 4:13)

The first question you must ask yourself is why you want to disciple your husband lovingly. Do you want to help him so you can have a great marriage? Though that is a good and biblical desire, it is not the primary reason for coming alongside him. Do you want to lovingly guide him because you want to make God's name great most of all? I trust that it is because that is the best reason (1 Corinthians 10:31). If your motive is not primarily for God's fame, you must do the necessary heart work before you go to the next step of working on your marriage. You may need to spend time with the Father to adjust your thinking for the challenging task ahead. Do not skip this vital step.

Ask God to give you the grace to love a not-so-lovable man. The Father will provide you with the favor if you ask with the right motive. Do not think God cannot perceive your heart's motives. He knows your intentions. You may be able to fool others by putting on a happy face and saying all the right words, but you cannot deceive God. If you think what I am asking you to do is more challenging than your ability to carry it out, you would be correct. God calls us to work beyond our ability, so we learn to stop relying on ourselves and choose to rely on Him, who can raise the dead (2 Corinthians 1:8–9).

Speaking with a spiritual leader in your local church would be best as you make the appropriate changes in your thinking. Do not be afraid to seek help. A courageous and wise Titus 2 mentor could prove invaluable. If you have humbly appealed to him to change and he has not repented, let him know you plan to speak with a church leader about these matters. You will not sin against him or God if you choose this course of action. But let me reiterate; whatever your course of action may be, you cannot sin against your husband. Perhaps this is where you should begin before you do anything else. And should you sin against him the next time he disappoints you, quickly repent to him and to God. You may be surprised at how your humility changes the environment in your home.

Call to Action

Every wife reading this is in a different place in their marriage. Let biblical wisdom rule your heart as you apply these truths to your life and marriage. For some of these women, their husbands are cruel, manipulative, and harmful. These ladies need to find help immediately because what I suggest here is not applicable.

1. What is the condition of your marriage? Is your husband teachable? Do you believe that God has regenerated him? No matter what he is today, do you think he has had a regenerative experience with God?
2. Why is it essential to know if your husband is born again, even if your assessment is subjectively derived?
3. Will you call upon the Spirit of God to work in his heart and make this your regular practice before you start applying these things in your marriage?
4. Who will you call on to help you think clearly about applying these truths? It's common for a wife to have cloudy judgment regarding her marriage. She's too close to it and desires change so badly that it can cloud her judgment, making it vital to have a clearer set of eyes helping her.
5. What one thing will you start doing today based on what you have read?

Setting Aside

8

Immature Husband

A lady asked, "Would you be willing to write about living with an immature husband and how to respond to him biblically? I need help; I would much appreciate it if you could give me some advice." Her question is not new to me. We are no longer a Christian society, a time when the Christian ethos was the zeitgeist, and it did not matter as much if you were a Christian because even the unregenerate culture had a clue what it meant to be a man. That day has passed. We have reared several generations where boys grow up with no biblically male templates that show them what it means to be good husbands.

Biff and Mable

Biff is immature and insecure. If Mable says anything related to him, their marriage, or his need to change, Biff takes it personally and usually sulks for days. Mable doesn't believe she can be candid with him because of his insecurity, fueling his pity parties and passive-aggressive responses. Mable chooses guardedness over openness whenever she is around him. Rather than speaking honestly about what is going on in her life, Mable reluctantly treats her husband like a child. She does not want to do this, but she is all too familiar with his infantile reactions when interacting with her concerns (John 16:12). Every word has to be measured and weighed before sharing it.

Mable is left to care for her soul while gingerly caring for Biff. She is pulling double duty. It is as though Mable has to grow him up before he can contribute to her sanctification appreciably. Though she can mature in Christ without him, there is a biblical presumption that husbands and wives cooperate in mutual sanctification. Biff is not cooperating, and Mable is missing out on this means of grace that would be an asset to her life and marriage. She tries not to be self-righteous about their awkward interactions, but it is hard. Biff is a fragile, immature, and insecure man. Mable wants to know how to move forward redemptively. Let me suggest seven considerations anyone could apply to their life and marriage, whether it's the wife or husband seeking guidance.

Is Biff a Christian?

One of the first things to consider is whether Biff is a Christian. I would not assume he is a Christian just because he says he is. It's not an uncharitable judgment of him but a typical starting place when trying to understand why someone is not changing. You must carefully assess him while holding your assessments loosely because you could be wrong. Even your best assessments will be subjective because we cannot know if someone is a believer. It is a reasonable assumption to think a person is a Christian if he attends a local church, hangs out with other Christians, or speaks the Christian vocabulary. As you try to discern whether he is a child of God, think on these three things.

GROWTH: I'm assuming you have known him for a while. If you could plot his spiritual growth on a chart, would you see steady upward growth? Has he been changing and maturing over the past decade? Let's say he has been changing. If so, how would you answer these questions? Has his growth been because of his interaction with the

Word of God and the Holy Spirit or because he has been learning Christian behaviors? Is he changing at the heart level—the control center for his behaviors—or is he merely learning new ideas, best practices, and valuable tips?

ILLUMINATION: Does Biff get spiritual things? Does he have discernment? I'm not asking if he is always right in his assessments because none of us are, but does he have spiritual insight? The Spirit of God illuminates the Christian mind, which is how we are enabled to see and discern spiritual things (1 Corinthians 2:14). There is a difference between interacting with a spiritually dense person and a spiritually discerning person. What I am talking about here is biblical maturity, regardless of age. Is he regularly illuminated and directed by the Spirit of God?

HUNGER: Does Biff thirst for God? Is God in his thoughts? Does he gravitate toward the ways of the Lord? Does Biff talk about what God is doing in his life? Is he learning things because he has thought about living in God's world? Is there a progression in his thoughts about God, life, and others? I'm asking if he is always stuck on the same old thing, or is he maturing—progressively moving forward in his sanctification. Does he like to talk to God? Are his prayers fresh, evolving, and alive? A divining rod gravitates toward the water. What does Biff gravitate toward to satisfy himself? If the Spirit is inside him, there should be a compelling desire to gravitate toward spiritual things. Describe his hunger for the things of God.

CAVEAT: You are not looking for perfection in any of the three things—growth, illumination, or hunger. You're looking for the presence of them. None of us have perfected our walk with God, but there should be objective evidence that we have been born from above.

Is Biff in Sin?

There are only two reasons a person will not mature in Christ according to his God-given character, capacities, and competencies. Either he is not a Christian, or he has a sin in his life. If he is a believer, it's a sin problem, so he is not changing. If sin has captured him, the Spirit of God cannot cooperate with him to help him mature (Romans 1:18; Ephesians 4:30; 1 Thessalonians 5:19; James 4:6). Typically, with a man, the most common secret sin is lust—of some sort. I think most women would be amazed to know how many men struggle this way. Do you know what he is looking at on the Internet? Do you have access to his phone, passwords, and other portals where he can access shameful things?

While I don't want to set off unnecessary alarms, I also don't want to assume everything is okay when dealing with a person like Biff. Something is wrong, and you must consider all the options. The simplest way to discern hidden sin is to ask him, and if you do ask him, how does he respond? His response will more than likely tell you what you need to know. You probably have your answer if he is defensive, angry, resistant, or seeks to avoid your inquiry. A humble man will respond humbly. If there is no secret sin, there is no reason for him to be uptight regarding your queries—assuming he knows you are for him, care for him, and are in the habit of loving and respecting him.

He Has Limited Authority

Your husband does not have absolute authority over you. If he is sinning and you both can't work it out, you need to find help, which is the point of Matthew 18:15-17. It would not be love to let him stay in his sin. You can humbly appeal to him to seek help through your local church. If he is a Christian and can't escape a lousy habit pattern, he should be willing to get help, and you should not be passive in trying to help him. Be careful here. Each situation is different. If you can talk to Biff, it would be wise to speak to him, but if you can't talk to Biff, ask the Father about the next steps. If you're in a sound local church, go to your pastor. Do not walk this path alone. If you have no church, ask the Father for one biblical relationship to come alongside you.

You Can't Change Him

Ultimately, God grants the gift of repentance (2 Timothy 2:24-26). I'm sure you know you cannot force righteousness. You cannot make anyone change. If Biff turns toward God, it will be because God has done a work in his heart (Proverbs 21:1). The hard part for you is not knowing when or if that will ever happen. If he does not change, there will be a need for significant work in your heart. A clunky marriage may be your cross as you wait, pray, and seek to serve Biff, hoping God will change him.

Examine Your Log

> Why do you see the speck that is in your brother's eye, but do not notice the log that is in your own eye? Or how can you say to your brother, "Let me take the speck out of your eye," when there is the log in your own eye? You hypocrite, first take the log out of your own eye, and then you will see clearly to take the speck out of your brother's eye.
>
> (Matthew 7:3-5)

No matter what you are dealing with regarding your husband, from your perspective and how you understand what Christ has done for you, it's imperative to know there is no stratification of humans—for all have sinned (Romans 3:10-12, 23; 1 Timothy 1:15). I do not say these things lightly. I've dealt with a few disappointing people: an abusive dad, two murdered brothers, and an unfaithful wife. The most effective means of grace in guarding my heart against bitterness and other forms of anger was discerning this fundamental truth: my sin against Christ was worse than anything done to me. If you understand and apply this truth correctly, you'll be able to be part of the solution rather than the problem. If there is a temptation to look down on him (Luke 18:11) because of what he has done wrong, your heart will take you to a bad place.

> Every conflict that comes into our lives has somehow been ordained by God. Knowing that he has personally tailored the events of our lives and is looking out for us at every moment should dramatically affect the way we respond to conflict.
> —Ken Sande

> Your attitude about someone will be your first clue as to your thoughts regarding that person, which will determine your actions toward them.
> —Rick Thomas

Model the Savior

Whatever it is you want Biff to be, you must become a representative of that for him. It would be disingenuous to insist that Biff be mature when you are not. Your modeling of Christ must always precede your teaching about Christ. Be careful about telling Biff how to behave when you're not acting according to your instruction. You're shooting yourself in the foot if you are not doing this. Do you want Biff to be humble? You show him humility. Do you want Biff to be honest with you? Be honest with him as much as possible while discerning his ability to steward what you want to say. Do you want Biff to encourage you? You encourage him.

Lead Your Husband

> *Though he was in the form of God . . . [He] emptied himself, by taking the form of a servant, being born in the likeness of men . . . He humbled himself by becoming obedient to the point of death, even death on a cross. Therefore God has highly exalted him and bestowed on him the name that is above every name.*
>
> (Philippians 2:5–9)

One of the most profound demonstrations and motivating examples of the gospel in a marriage is when a spouse sets aside their desires for the greater good of the other person. Isn't that what the Savior did for us? Jesus set aside the life He enjoyed with the Father to come to earth to help us become what we couldn't be on our own. His example is our call (1 Peter 2:18–25). We are to emulate this setting aside for the redemptive good of others (Philippians 2:3). It is easy for a wife to lose a gospel focus and application in her marriage. Instead of working toward maturing the marriage through Christ-mirrored humility, she lowers herself to anger by making demands. Of course, it is even more challenging when her desires are not evil (Luke 22:42), one of the hardest things for us to emulate about Christ. The call to die to ourselves is impossibly hard (Luke 9:23).

Call to Action

The questions throughout this chapter are challenging but necessary. Will you work through them? They come with a prayer for God's soothing mercy to caress your soul as you take it to task. You're in the most demanding spot, and I'm sad for you and your husband. As with all hard places comes difficult questions. I trust you can receive these truth-directed questions with a spirit of love.

1. Jesus set aside His desires for the greater good of you and me. In what ways can you model the example of Christ in your marriage?
2. Do you know how to serve your husband this way? Do you want to do this for him?
3. What needs to change in you to cooperate more practically with the Lord in the sanctification of your immature husband?
4. Will you seek help from the body of Christ?

There are many wives who do not have husbands who lead well. God is calling them to do one of the hardest things they could do—submit to someone who does not want to care for them biblically. It's a painful place to be. The best you can do is model what I have outlined here. If you do, albeit imperfectly, I promise you will experience a persevering grace from the Lord. He provides mercy for the humble, your best action in an unchangeable situation.

9

Power of Unforgiveness

Sometimes in some relationships, a person will utilize unforgiveness as a tool for self-protection. They weaponize unforgiveness, even if they do so unwittingly. They might hold on to unforgiveness because they have been hurt so many times by the same person, usually a spouse. They are frustrated and disappointed and believe there is no other recourse but a self-reliant means of self-protection. Suppose you sense this is happening with a friend. In that case, you must tread courageously and carefully as you help them see how they are complicating—even self-sabotaging—an already complicated matter.

Self-Prescribed Cancer

When forgiveness is the right option, but the hurt person chooses unforgiveness, it could be a false security measure to protect themselves from future suffering. It won't work, at least long-term. The person holding on to the anger and hurt cannot see (or is unwilling to see) how unforgiveness is self-prescribed cancer; it will eat away at their unforgiving soul. Their unforgiveness suggests two things: "I will not let you close to hurt me again, and I will not let you be free from what you did." It is both protective and punitive. No one should hold on to any sin, no matter how justified or insecure they feel. They must understand that unforgiveness is a form of anger that will take revenge on the soul. It will tangle their soul in knots (Galatians 6:1) as they punish those who have hurt them (Luke 23:34).

Have you been tempted to withhold forgiveness from someone? If you have, the best thing to do is seek help from those who can walk you through letting go of self-punishment and punitive anger. No matter what has happened to you, holding on to anger and unforgiveness will wear you down to a nub. It is as unwise as it is un-gospel, something our friends—Biff and Mable—learned the hard way. Their marriage was your typical looks-okay-on-the-outside relationship. But the inside was full of loneliness and low-grade hostility toward each other—until all hell broke loose, the day the tables turned, and Mable became empowered by unforgiveness.

Biff was a likable guy. Every time they went to counseling, he and the counselor hit it off, which would infuriate Mable. It was one of the reasons she stopped going. She later said, "Why go? He will go, put on his people-pleasing smile, and the counselor will wonder why I have a problem within twenty minutes. They like Biff because everybody likes Biff. They come to the same conclusion: he married a nagging discontent. So why bother?" The consensus was that his perceived spiritual maturity and humble servant's heart were something others should emulate. When he wasn't running his moderately successful business, he volunteered at his local church, leading not one but two men's Bible studies. The pastors loved him because he was free labor, and they saw Biff as a model Christian.

Spilled the Beans

It didn't help that they were too busy to look beyond the surface of his life. "Besides, the squeaky wheel gets the grease," and Biff never squeaked. Except for one glaring problem: Mable could not stand Biff. It was their hidden marital secret. She had lived with a low-grade hatred toward her husband for nearly twenty years. The only reasons she would not leave him were the stigma of divorce—"what it would do to their children"—the hassle of starting over, or "God hates divorce, you know," she said sarcastically. Mable's issue with Biff was pretty straightforward: he was a hypocrite. Biff was a self-absorbed people-pleaser who learned how to manage the gap between who he was and the person he presented himself to be. The problem for Biff and Mable was that he could not maintain his hypocrisy entirely, and as these things tend to go, the one place where he could not keep up a front was in his home.

That was okay with Biff. Mostly. He counted on Mable not to spill the beans, and Mable acquiesced because living in a lie was the path of least resistance. With no public chink in his spiritual armor, she silently suffered through it all. Though she had an occasional short fuse, in the depths of her heart, she knew something more sinister was in play. Give a hypocrite an inch, and he'll take a mile. The problem was that she could not pinpoint where it all led. Coupled with this low-grade anger toward him was her fear that whatever he was into would devastate her. That awareness gave her another reason not to look too deeply into Biff's life. For her, ignorance was an uncomfortable but acceptable bliss.

It was late on a Monday afternoon when Mable emptied the home office trashcan that she noticed a receipt from a strip club. It was unmistakable. Her heart beat furiously, and her mouth went dry. Her ignorance became knowledge, and the news crushed her soul. Her tension was between walking out the door for good and confronting Biff with the truth she found in the trash. She chose to engage, and not surprisingly, Biff was shocked, though he quickly regained his equilibrium and went into his people-pleasing routine. Mable was not impressed; she had seen that shtick too many times. She stood firm. After a few days of drawn-out arguments, denials, confrontations, and threats, Biff finally came clean.

The Wounded's Weapon

He told Mable what she later recalled as the worst news of her life. He was into porn. She was devastated. In time, Biff went to counseling and came completely clean about his sin. Remarkably he chose not to stick with his well-worn people-pleasing routine, and he received favor from the Lord (James 4:6), which gave him what he needed to walk out repentance. Biff always wanted to be free from his sin. He later said he was glad it came out because he did not have the integrity or the courage to let others know how he struggled. Mable, on the other hand, was struggling. Even a year later, she was unwilling to forgive Biff. Mable was angry, critical, bitter, self-justifying, and self-righteous. Twelve months later, she would not let it go in her heart or marriage. Mable had been hurting for two decades. Twenty years! She also had been stewing in anger for most of that time.

From her perspective, forgiveness seemed too easy for Biff. Even when others made heartfelt appeals for her to let it go, she would not relent. She knew she was right—or wanted others to believe she was. She felt people did not understand. How could they? They did not live with Biff, and only a few knew the soul-rending effect porn could have on a spouse. She saw Biff for who he was—a hypocritical fool, which soured her belief in his genuine repentance. As she said, "He did not willingly confess his sins; I caught him!"

She believed he probably would never have confessed his sin if she had not found the strip club receipt. She was more than likely correct. Biff even said as much. Though he wanted help, he was too weak in his faith to trust God enough with the most powerful and darkest secret of his life. Plus, he enjoyed his shiny Christian reputation.

Mable did say that she had forgiven him, but there was nothing in her attitude and actions that would support her claim. During counseling, Mable's counselor talked to her about her unwillingness to forgive. The actual truth eventually came out: her belief that she lived alone her entire marriage and that God never intervened in the nightmare. Mable was hurt and felt it wasn't proportionally equitable to forgive after a year when she repeatedly suffered for two decades. The more sinister side of Mable believed that if she forgave Biff for his sin, it would be like he never sinned. From her perspective, he would get off free and clear, and the door of her nightmare would close as though it had never happened. That was not tenable for Mable. She was bitter and not ready to forget her hurt. In some ways, her hurt was a form of security. It was a reminder that kept her vigilant about what a person could do to her. She was like an institutionalized convict who couldn't live in any other place but the prison of unforgiveness.

Power of Unforgiveness

Biff indeed repented of his sin even though he did not initially confess it. Once it was in the open, he admitted everything. (See David's lack of confession until confronted by Nathan in 2 Samuel 12:1-12, Psalm 32:1-4, and Psalm 51:1-19). Mable was not impressed by his remorse and was unwilling to let him off the hook. She knew enough about God and the gospel to realize that forgiving someone was like saying,

I will obey God and forgive you for your sin regardless of what you have done to me. Because the power of forgiveness neutralizes the sin, we will work on the damage done. I realize that what I have done to my Savior is far worse than what you have done to me or could ever do to me, even though what you have done to me has been devastating.

Nevertheless, I will not hold this over your head any longer, but I will make myself vulnerable to the Lord, knowing that you could hurt me again. In essence, I trust God's sovereign care over my life and His method of conflict resolution rather than my own. I choose to be obedient to Him. I forgive you.

Her unwillingness to forgive Biff was a common-sense, man-centered way of protecting herself—an understandable temptation (1 Corinthians 1:25). Though she would not say it, Mable believed she would not be vulnerable as long as she could hold Biff's sin over his head. She was not grasping how her unforgiveness was forcing her head under the waters of bitterness. The power of the gospel is freely extending forgiveness to offenders either transactionally or attitudinally. The power of unforgiveness is choosing not to release yourself—attitudinally—or the other person—transactionally—from what happened. Mable essentially was saying that since God did not come through for her for twenty years, she would take matters into her hands. Her self-protective shield of unforgiveness was an attempt to accomplish three things:

- She was punishing Biff for all the years he punished her.
- She was protecting herself from ever being hurt again. (Of course, she was not protecting herself at all.)
- She was perverting the gospel.

Power of the Gospel

Sin disorients and distorts our thinking. Sin does not let God be God but entices us to assume the role of godness. Mable was playing god. She was holding Biff's sin over his head while mocking the cross. The Father's punishment of His Son on the cross was insufficient for Mable. While genuinely believing the gospel, she could not fully embrace its cleansing and freeing power. Grace seemed too easy. What Mable did not understand fully is that grace has never been effortless. For her to have the grace to forgive, it cost Jesus Christ His life. The infinite Father punished the Son for an infinite crime. The Savior paid an infinite price for the infinite crime. Biff and Mable received infinite forgiveness for their infinite crimes. Mable was unwilling to accept the death of Christ as a sufficient payment to cover Biff's sins.

She was treating her husband in a way that God did not treat her when she asked for forgiveness for the crimes she committed against Him. The irony in this story is that Biff is free as he walks out repentance, but Mable is in prison. Forgiving Biff does not say that what he did to her does not matter. It also does not let him off the hook because Biff needs help. Sin had captured him for many years (Galatians 6:1-3), and temptation continues to lure him into sin. If Mable wants to keep from being hurt again, she must work to do it God's way and forgive him. Being his enemy worsens matters, complicating his temptation, their marriage, and her soul. Forgiving Biff will release both of them from what has been hindering them while positioning them to begin the process of actual restoration.

Call to Action

1. Who has hurt you? What did they do? How do you think about them? Are you free from what they did, or do you continue to harbor a sinful attitude toward them?
2. Are you holding onto any unforgiveness toward anyone? If so, what does unforgiveness reveal about your understanding of the gospel?
3. Will you talk about the irony of an offending person being free from their sin, but the victim of their sin continues to harbor sin because of what happened to them?
4. Do you see how unforgiveness hinders receiving the help the offended needs and hinders the offender's need to mature in Christ?
5. If you're hurting from what someone did to you, will you find help today to begin walking through any unwillingness to forgive—either attitudinally or transactionally—the person who hurt you?

10

Need to Forgive

Sometimes you can forgive someone for their sin against you and reconcile with them. It's a beautiful picture of the power of the gospel. Other times you can forgive them, but you won't be able to reconcile with them, another picture, albeit incomplete, of the gospel. The first forgiveness opportunity is transactional, while the second is attitudinal—in your heart. Either way, you can experience freedom from the sin of others if you will forgive. The best case is transactional, where both parties experience freedom, but sometimes all you can do is forgive them in your heart.

Will You Forgive?

Marriage counseling is the most common type of help sought within the Christian community. Most of these couples come because they are willing to work through the struggles between them. They want help and are eager to work together. These couples are more straightforward to help because they want to be on the same marital page. They are not biting and devouring one another, as Paul would say. There is a maturity about them and mutual recognition that there is work to do for both. Then there are the other couples who bring issues to you, but it's more complicated. They are not pulling in the same direction but working against each other. These complex couples represent a higher degree of difficulty because they are not on the same marital page and are less desirous of reconciling.

Ironically, God's grace is sufficient for both sets because His Word can sift through the problems and bring resolution. (See 2 Corinthians 12:9; 1 Corinthians 10:13; 2 Timothy 3:16–17; Amos 3:3.) The key to discerning the second couple's lack of desire to reconcile ties almost always to one of the spouse's unwillingness to forgive the other person. Without forgiveness, you cannot reconcile with someone attitudinally and transactionally. Attitudinal forgiveness is an attitude of forgiveness that releases someone from the management of what the other person did. Minimally, the offended person can forgive the offending spouse in their heart. Transactional forgiveness is when the perpetrator comes to you and transacts forgiveness by asking you to release them from their sin.

There is a complexity in a spouse's heart when she comes to marriage counseling to reconcile with her husband but is unwilling to forgive (attitudinal or transactional) her husband for what he has done. In such cases, the wife has set up an impossible problem to solve. There is an uncomfortable truth operative here: you cannot move toward reconciliation with your spouse if you are unwilling to forgive—at least attitudinally. Minimally, you must be willing to release the other person in your heart from what they did to you. Some spouses attempt to maintain a posture of unforgiveness while reconciling. It's as logical as slashing your wrist and expecting not to bleed or jumping off a ten-story building while anticipating you will not hurt. A spouse must first decide if she will forgive her husband.

Intellectually Dishonest

Some years ago, I was counseling a couple like this. The wife was furious at her husband. Simultaneously holding onto her anger and unforgiveness, she expected me to fix her marriage. It reminded me of the parent of an angry teen illustration. The parent is trying to get the rebellious teen to sit down. The angry teen refuses. Then the parent makes the teen sit by force. The teen sits but defiantly says, "You can make me sit down on the outside, but I'm standing up on the inside." This attitude is the way some spouses are. They are not honest with themselves, God, their spouses, or their counselor. They are trying to have the best of both worlds. They do not want to let go of their unforgiveness while perplexed at why they can't have a reconciled marriage. You can't sit down and stand up simultaneously; you can't have it both ways. The four most common responses when a spouse tries to justify or explain their unforgiveness, though she rarely admits the intellectual dishonesty in her heart, are as follows.

- "I can forgive, but I can't forget."
- "You can be angry and not sin. The Bible says so."
- "You don't know what he has done to me."
- "I love him, but I don't like him."

At best, these deceptions are devoid of the gospel. At worst, it is willful deceit. Without a doubt, it is a hurt spouse unwilling to apply the gospel to their situation, or worse, they do not want to implement the gospel to their marriage problems. I am not marginalizing what a sinful person has done to them. To trivialize or overlook suffering would not embrace the compassion of the Savior or recognize the necessity of the gospel. The gospel implies that sin is real, damaging, hurtful, and hard to change. But if you want to reconcile with your spouse, you must do some of the hardest things God has ever called you to do. First, you will have to take your soul to task to determine if you want to focus on the reconciliation process while moving toward reconciliation goals. You cannot reconcile while giving most of your mental space to what someone did to you.

A Reconciling Heart

Being sin-centered is not the way of the Savior. Jesus fixed His heart upon the cross—a posture that He calls all His children to emulate. He was thinking about how He could die for another person's sins. He had a reconciling heart, not an unforgiving one. His point of focus was not primarily on what individuals did to Him but on how He could reconcile a broken and sinful people to His Father. What is the fixation of your heart: to reconcile a captured person (Galatians 6:1-2) to God or to keep what they did to you in the front of your mind at all times? Christ never avoided, ignored, or highlighted what sin had done to His creation. He wept over Jerusalem and Lazarus, and He carried much sorrow in His heart over what you and I have done to Him. He never overlooked the problem of sin and how the complexities of sinfulness have disrupted the divine community of Father, Son, and Spirit (Philippians 2:6-7).

Do you want to be Christlike? If so, God calls you to forgive your spouse—attitudinally or transactionally—so you can move toward reconciliation (1 Peter 2:18-25). You can do this because the gospel is not an unforgiving gospel. The gospel is a reconciling gospel. Thus, what you want to address here is your point of focus: what can you do to forgive, or what did someone do to you? This intersection in your life is a marriage-shaping, future-altering, and God-honoring question. Take time to ask yourself: what am I more about regarding my life with God and others? While I'm not asking you to ignore what your spouse did to you as though it does not matter, I am asking where you are primarily directing your heart. If you have a reconciling heart, you will desire to do these four things:

- You will not only forgive but also put a proactive plan of forgetting into practice, just like your Savior did for you.
- You will be honest with your anger by accurately assessing your heart and pursuing God with heartbroken repentance.
- You will realize that what you have done to your Savior is a million times, to the tenth power—ad infinitum—worse than what anyone has ever done or will ever do to you.
- You will stop splitting hairs between love and like to justify your unwillingness to reconcile. Semantical rigamarole obscures reality.

Shallow Defenses

The Savior loves you, and He likes you, not because you have merited His affection but because He is a reconciling friend. Your sin does not overpower His love for or His liking of you. A reconciling person would not make false intellectual assertions because they don't focus on the sin committed but on the grace appropriated through the gospel. Let me track back through all four of them, making a gospel application that I trust will assist any wayward offended heart to seek to align themselves to the potential and power of the gospel.

- "I can forgive, but I can't forget" pinpoints the sin committed, not the power of the gospel. The sin-centered soul will not see the cross of Christ with the clarity they need to be free from what happened to them.
- "I can be angry and not sin" focuses on the evil

committed—what I can be mad about—rather than what the gospel can do for the sin committed. It's an eisegetical reading of Scripture to support a punitive heart.
- "You don't know what he has done to me" is dialed in on the sin committed while marginalizing the healing power of the gospel. While not trivializing what happened to you, we must measure all offenses in the light of our transgressions against God.
- "I love him, but I don't like him" is a cutesy, semantical way to focus on a person's sin while ignoring the redemptive power of the gospel. I hope this person has enough self-awareness to see such shallow resistance to the gospel's power.

All four of these assertions slant the heart of the person—who has been hurt—on what happened to them while pushing the gospel to the periphery of their marriage. Reconciliation cannot occur when these things are lingering or festering in the heart. These intellectually dishonest assertions are only an issue for a person struggling with unforgiveness. If you are leaning into reconciliation, you will not make these assertions. While they may exist in your heart—because you are human—God's grace is more extraordinary than our shallow resistance toward forgiveness.

Intentional Forgetfulness

You do not have to tell the reconciling heart how to forgive or forget. The reconciling heart pursues forgiveness and grace-empowered forgetfulness. Yes, such a person will struggle, especially with deliberate, intentional forgetfulness, but the grace in her heart will overpower temptations toward falling back into those traps. Pursuing forgetfulness does not mean you will develop amnesia. It means you will choose not to bring it up punitively. Omniscient God can never forget any sin we have perpetrated against Him or others. Not remembering something would take away from His all-knowing, making Him less than Himself. Impossible. Our great and gracious God chooses never to bring up what we have done in a punitive, "get back at you" way. He can do this because He has punished the sin through His Son. The crime is not being neglected, overlooked, or marginalized.

- God is hurt more by the sin of your spouse than you are.
- God takes the sin of your spouse more seriously than you do.
- God is more forgiving than you could imagine regarding your spouse's sin.
- God has done more to reconcile sinful people to Himself than you could ever do.

The best news is that He mercifully gives you the grace to do similarly—toward those who sin against you. It's your choice. You will know if you have this kind of grace in your heart to the degree that it does not control your thinking and tempt you to sin. If you can't do this, the problem is not with what happened to you or who did what to you but your unwillingness to trust God by forgiving the person who sinned against you. If you will not apply God's all-sufficient grace to what someone did to you, it means that that person's sin keeps you from getting something you desire—something you crave more than you want forgiveness and reconciliation with God or them.

Unmet desires are the resisting forces with forgiveness. The only reason a person will withhold forgiveness is that the perpetrator of the transgression has disrupted, hindered, held back, or stolen something that the offended desired. The thing craved or desired is more significant than God's ability to make things right by His grace. Unforgiveness becomes the method of choice to make them pay for what they took. Regardless of your motive for withholding forgiveness, the result will be the same: there will be no possibility of reconciliation. You cannot hold onto your hurt, regardless of how painful it is or how disappointing what they did to you. Perhaps your spouse is not asking for forgiveness. It happens. The good news is that you can release yourself from what they did by forgiving them attitudinally—in your heart. It won't be transactional, and the person will not experience release from sin, but you can experience freedom from their evil.

Call to Action

1. What are attitudinal and transactional forgiveness? How do they differ?
2. Will you write out or talk through two scenarios, one with attitudinal and the other with transactional forgiveness? You must understand both.
3. Are you in a situation currently where the transgressor is not asking you to transact forgiveness with them? If so, why is it essential for you to forgive them in your heart? What will it do to your soul to release them in your heart?
4. Two people in a conflict do not work through it equally or at the same pace because they are at different places with the Lord. In some cases, it might take an offender years to get to transactional forgiveness if they ever get there. Regardless, you do not have to be in their prison if you're willing to forgive them attitudinally.

11

A Harsh Husband

Harshness is one of the most typical forms of anger, and the most common context for it is within a family construct, especially between a husband and wife. When you put two or more sinners in a box for an extended period, their rawest Adamic tendencies will be impossible to hide. Dating is great, but living together forever increases the possibilities of sin exponentially. I trust these seven considerations will help if you're married to a harsh person.

1: God Loves You

As I share these seven essentials, will you consider a few complexities, especially if the harsh person is a husband. For example, more than likely, the wife has no grounds for divorce. Also, God calls her to submit to her husband while expecting her not to sin against him in return. Unfortunately, in too many situations, it could be a while before she sees any changes in him, making a marriage like this heartbreaking. Whenever the Lord calls me to help a struggling wife, I feel like the doctor who has to tell his patient terrible news. I wish I could change her marriage, but I know that I cannot; my call is to water and plant while pleading with the Lord to bring the needed transformation.

I realize it's a short step for her from trusting and resting in the Lord to thinking God is distant and silent. Unmitigated suffering can change our attitude toward the Lord. We pray, appeal, plead, and beg, but our circumstances do not improve. In time, we can quickly think the Lord does not care and is uninvolved (Job 23:2-5). Drifting from God is a simpler temptation than you might think. There is a vacuum in a dysfunctional marriage that keeps you alone, even when you are in a crowd. If you are not careful, you can begin to think the good Lord has left you too. It is not true.

Thus, the first thing I want a struggling wife to know is that God loves her, and her circumstances do not alter His love. Conditions can change us, but one of the Lord's many attributes is His immutability; He never changes (Malachi 3:6; Hebrews 13:8). She must preach the gospel to herself every day. If you are in a situation like this, repeat after me: "God loves me and proved His love by sending His Son to die on the cross (John 3:16). Jesus paid for my sins, and I am eternally secure, even though my marriage is not all I hoped it would be (John 10:28-30)." It's tempting to lose sight of God's love, making this assurance the first thing to remind yourself of when the person you married is not loving you well.

2: Sin Captures

The word Adam means "red man" or "man of the earth" (Genesis 2:7). Adam is a dirt clod, and so is the harsh husband. For the record, all of us are dirt clods, no exceptions. When the Lord looked down on His creation in Psalm 103:14, He remembered that we are dust. There is a fragility and vulnerability to humankind—we are jars of clay (2 Corinthians 4:7). Then, after you mix the doctrine of sin (Genesis 3:7) into our pre-made clay containers, we are a mess (Romans 3:10-12). Harsh husbands are a particular kind of mess. Without condescension, it would do your soul well to recognize he's a mess, no matter what you think of him or how he tries to present himself. He is a vulnerable, depraved mess who cannot maintain any sustained goodness apart from the grace of God.

> Brothers, if anyone is caught in any transgression, you who are spiritual should restore him in a spirit of gentleness. Keep watch on yourself, lest you too be tempted. Bear one another's burdens, and so fulfill the law of Christ. For if anyone thinks he is something, when he is nothing, he deceives himself.
> (Galatians 6:1-3)

Paul would say sin has caught your husband. Imagine walking through the woods and finding your husband ensnared by a bear trap around the ankle. That is what Paul is saying. Sin caught your husband, who cannot extricate himself from it without your help. Captured by sin is a fundamental understanding, which should lead you to pity him as you think about his frame (Psalm 103:14)—that he is from the dust impregnated by sin (Genesis 2:7, 3:6; Romans 5:12). His incarceration does not excuse his sin but should motivate you to gently confront him.

3: You Must Restore

Understanding his fallenness is where you must think seriously about how you want to respond to him. How would you react if you walked up on him in the forest? Would you become angry with him or try to restore him gently? Read what Paul is asking you to do in Galatians 6:1-3. Humbly responding to Paul's teaching is one of the most demanding applications of the gospel a person could ever make: submitting yourself to the sins of others. Think Christ here. He gave Himself up for us, the caught ones. I am not saying you should submit to physical harm. That is another discussion. You should never subject yourself to violence.

4: Find Help

Because your husband's habituation is in a pattern of harshness and you are vulnerable, you must reach out for help. Do not go through this alone. Regardless of his desire to control you through his manipulations or attempts at reputation management, you find someone to help you both walk through this process. Submission to him does not prevent you from helping him. If sin has captured him, you must help him. You can submit to him and help him at the same time. One of the aspects of submission is respect, and if you do not help him, you do not respect him.

You can substitute the word love for respect. If you love him, you will help him. Again, you can do this while submitting to him. Lucia and I have asked our children to do this for us. When they experience our sinfulness, we ask them to question our words and behaviors. Submission to us and speaking into our lives do not negate each other. Only a twisted view of submission would teach otherwise. Our children live in those dual roles of submission and equality, as well as my wife. We are equally made in the image of God and equally of the same status in the body of Christ, though we have different roles in our relationships.

5: The Long Haul

There is a good chance your husband will never change to your complete satisfaction. I do not know if he will, and I am unsure if the Lord wants him to change. I do know there are scores of situations in the Bible where the Lord allowed sin while using it in a sinless way. One example is Paul's thorn in the flesh (2 Corinthians 12:7–10). The story of Joseph is another example (Genesis 50:20), as is the life of Pharaoh (Exodus 9:16; Romans 9:17). The most profound illustration of this is the gospel.

> *For our sake he made him to be sin who knew no sin, so that in him we might become the righteousness of God.*
>
> (2 Corinthians 5:21)

I am not saying this is the case for you, but it is not out of the realm of possibilities. Though it is counterintuitive to our native way of thinking (1 Corinthians 1:18), there are times when suffering is God's way of breaking us from our self-reliant tendencies (2 Corinthians 1:8-9). Notice how Paul talked about his suffering in Asia. He did not want folks to misunderstand why God was permitting their hardship. There will be times when our suffering is the perfect means for God to demonstrate His strength through us.

> *For we do not want you to be unaware, brothers, of the affliction we experienced in Asia. For we were so utterly burdened beyond our strength that we despaired of life itself. Indeed, we felt that we had received the sentence of death. But that was to make us rely not on ourselves but on God who raises the dead.*
>
> (2 Corinthians 1:8-9)

6: Unceasing Prayers

Though I am unsure your husband will change, there is no question the Lord is calling you to an other-worldly reliance on Him. Along with reminding yourself of the impossible, you must remind yourself of the possible. The impossible says, "I cannot change my husband." The possible says, "The Lord can change our relationship." If you only remind yourself of the impossible, you may become depressed and, thus, set up for temptations that will develop sin patterns in your life. As you remind yourself of the impossibility of the situation, be sure to transition quickly to making your supplications known to the Lord. Here are five ways you can pray.

- Ask the Father to change your husband.
- Ask the Father to change you.
- Give thanks to the Lord for your husband.
- Give thanks to the Lord for what He is teaching you.
- Give thanks to the Lord for random things.

Your gratitude will affect your attitude. I know it is a quirky saying, but you will remember it. Applying it to your life will change you regardless of what happens to your husband. If you are predisposed to journaling, I recommend you write your grateful thoughts each day as you present them to the Lord. Paul had a habit of being grateful for mean people: "I give thanks to my God always for you" (1 Corinthians 1:4).

7: Guard Your Heart

Finally, my sister, guard your heart with all diligence because what flows out of it will determine the course of your life (Proverbs 4:23; Luke 6:45). Your marriage may tempt you to sin because your disappointment is deep and complex. Here are five possible sin traps for you to consider while asking the Lord to fortify your heart so you don't fall into any of them.

1: ANGER: James 4:1-2 says anger connects to what we are not getting. The most practical way to repent of your anger is to identify what you are not getting or are afraid of losing. Whatever that thing is that you want will be the source (cause) of your anger. Ask the Spirit to reveal this to you and fight to eliminate it.

2: REVENGE: Part of your anger will be to inflict punishment on your husband. Carefully study yourself. Figure out how this temptation operates in your life. All of us are different, so how we react to others will vary. It may be good for you to talk with a close friend who is familiar with your situation and has the courage to help you identify how you may sin against your husband.

3: Self-Pity: Another form of anger is when you turn it away from your husband and onto yourself, which manifests in several ways. One of which is self-pity. Anger turned inward destroys the soul. It will eat you alive if you do not promptly take care of it, impacting your thoughts, emotions, and attitudes.

4: Regret: Another form of anger is disappointment, which ties to an insufficient understanding of the sovereignty of God. Regret is a ground-level, backward glance at life's circumstances, marginalizing sovereignty. Regret does not consider how God is in your mess or working redemptively to bring about purposes you cannot perceive now. Be careful here. Guard your heart. God is multitasking, and you must assume you are working with insufficient data.

5: Fear: Your fear can come at you from many angles. The opposite of fear is faith. The most oft-repeated appeal in the Bible is fear not. If you begin applying some of the things here, your fear will slowly morph into confidence in God's ability to do more than you could ask or think.

Call to Action

1. Do you believe that God is in your mess? Why did you answer that way, and what does it reveal about your relationship with Him?
2. How does the love of God buoy your soul during this time of marital challenges?
3. Of the five things listed under "guard your heart," will you rank them in order of most challenging to you, and what is one thing you will do to overcome these challenges?
4. As you think about sin capturing your husband, does it drive you to pity him while motivating you to want to come alongside him to help restore? Why did you answer that way?
5. Why is it okay to lead your husband while submitting to him? The answer is that your role is submission, but you are also a fellow image bearer God calls you to love well, including how you bring corrective care to him. What would this kind of care look like in your situation?
6. Who will you call on to help you restore your husband in a spirit of gentleness?

12

Disciple and Submit

One of the primary responsibilities of a wife is to disciple her husband. She is the number one sanctifying human agent in his life outside of himself, of course. Nobody knows more about him than she does. To disciple any person well, you must know them well, and who knows a husband better than his wife? She has seen him during his best days and experienced him on his worst days. What he does to keep others from knowing him is more apparent to her. Thus, the million-dollar question is, how does a wife provide soul care for her husband?

Equal and Subordinate

One of the Lord's advantages, which makes Him so practical in our lives, is His care for us, which flows from His knowledge about us (Psalm 139:1-4; Hebrews 4:12-13). In a similar—albeit finite—fashion, a wife has the inside scoop on her husband. She does not know all that God knows about him, but she knows more than anyone else. He may put his best foot forward in the public domain, but she is familiar with both feet.

Some people have confused biblical submission. The implication of their teaching is the wife is inferior to her husband. Nothing in God's Word supports this notion. A better view of a wife's role in marriage is like Christ in His humanness. He is co-equal with God as far as His "God-ness" is concerned, but He submitted to the Father as a human. This imperfect analogy works in a marriage. She is equal to her husband as far as her ontology. He has nothing on her that would make him better than her, but she is subordinate to him in her role in the marriage.

Equality and subordination are not at odds with each other in roles and relationships. It is similar to an employer. The employer is no better than the employee, but there is appropriate submission. It is the same for children. I am not better than our children, though I am their leader. I do not view them as inferior. They are children made in the image of God. Even babies in the womb have the full dignity of humanness and image-bearing. They are respected, loved, and honored just like any other human.

Lead from Behind

> If your brother sins against you, go and tell him his fault, between you and him alone. If he listens to you, you have gained your brother.
> (Matthew 18:15)

Roles and relationships do not have to compete with each other. Making the wife co-equal with her husband is an essential and proper aspect of discipleship. The wife is responsible for bringing biblical care to him. He is her brother. He needs her discipleship care because he struggles with sin like her. (See Romans 7:21–25 and 1 John 1:7–10.) If he is not her brother, he needs her evangelistic care. Either way, he needs her speaking into his life because sin is not "uninterested" in him.

Nobody has more contact with him, and nobody has more insight into his life. She must go into all the world making disciples, starting with herself as her primary disciplee (Matthew 28:19-20). Her husband comes next. She will have to come to terms with her discipleship responsibility. Leading someone while subordinate to them is an everyday opportunity that does not have to feel like being in front, demanding others follow.

Yelling at while waving people forward creates robot followers, not mature Christians. It may be helpful for a subordinate follower to make a distinction between leading and leadership. Leading, narrowly defined, is an assigned task that expects followers to follow to accomplish an expectation, e.g., a teacher might single out a child to lead the group to the cafeteria. Leadership is more comprehensive and nuanced. It does not have to mean being in front.

Counter-intuitive Leader

Jesus led by washing people's feet (John 13:1-17). He led by giving His life to others (Mark 10:45). He taught a counter-intuitive leadership model (Matthew 20:16). Some people only see leading in a single-dimensioned way, the painted-faced squadron leader taking the hill with his loyal troops scrambling up behind him. This perspective is a potentially skewed view of leadership. I cannot help but wonder how many Christian women realize the leadership power they possess. How many of them know how to leverage their leadership ability in the lives of their husbands?

If they have any view of leadership at all, it is the either/or belief that our culture believes: I'm either in charge of you, or I submit to you; I will dominate or become a mindless follower. This kind of illogicalness creates leadership competition within the marriage. The husband fights with his wife for the home's leadership (wrongly defined). His wife will fight back because she does not want his poor treatment of her.

He feels his wife's resistance and ratchets his efforts to

take charge. If he is less tenacious, he will quit leading by abdicating his role. Either way, he will lose: his wife will fight him toe-to-toe, or she will disrespect him for being a wuss. The Bible does not teach these forms of leadership, which is our competitive culture speaking, not God's Word. There is a more effective way for wives to bless their husbands. Let me address nine of them.

Nine Ways to Discipline Him

1: GET A BURDEN: (Galatians 6:1) Every wife has a "caught husband." He is not entirely sanctified. The Bible does not teach sinless perfection. Every husband has sin struggles like everyone else. Every wife should pray for a burden for her husband if she does not have one already. She does this because she wants to honor the Lord by not missing out on the opportunities to help him in his sanctification. She knows marriage is more about what she can pour into it than what she can get out of it, a sign of an effective leader. Will there be benefits of esteeming others more? Of course. Read Philippians 2:1–11.

2: PRAY FOR HIM: (1 Corinthians 1:4) Prayer is a great way to access the Trinity on behalf of the sanctification of a husband. Maybe the Lord will change him, a strong reason a wife wants to pray. In addition to asking for things, she wants to thank God for her husband. I think about how Paul prayed for the Corinthians. He spent time thanking God for those mean folks. Paul had an extravagant love for them, which paved the way for him to correct them. If a wife does not have affection for the person she wants to help, the help she offers may blow up on her. Perhaps her first prayer will be to change her heart toward her husband.

3: MODEL YOUR GOAL: (Philippians 4:9) An excellent exercise is for her to write out the things she would like for her husband to become. Here are a few examples: humble, servant, encourager, respectful, loving, kind, gentle, and passionate about God. These few things will make any marriage sing. A core tenet of biblical leadership is to become the person you want others to be. To think otherwise is hypocritical and destructive to any relationship. Expecting or demanding someone to be what we are not is wrong. To lead well is to show them what to become by our others-centered, God-honoring example (Ephesians 5:1; 1 Corinthians 11:1).

4: WIN WITH ENCOURAGEMENT: (Ephesians 4:29) She must ensure her words have a "building up effect" rather than a corrupting, tearing down one. A word fitly spoken can transform anyone's world while the "unfitly spoken word" will destroy it (Proverbs 25:11). We have power in our words. A wife can draw her husband to herself and Christ by what she says or push him farther away. One of the most effective assessment questions a spouse can ask is, "What do you experience more from me: my encouragement or my displeasure?" If she wants to lead her husband well, she will have to be courageous and grace-filled enough to check her blind spots. She can do this by asking him about his experience with her.

5: MAKE IT EASY: (Genesis 3:7) Husbands are proud, self-reliant people who do not want to show weakness. I know this because I am one. We men like to pretend we are strong and impenetrable. Throw in a little sin and what you get is a person who does not want to reveal his flaws, especially to his wife. He wants to impress, which makes a wife's condemnation and criticism of him acuter. Perhaps he has given up on impressing her. It is not hopeless; it means she has more leadership work to do. One of the Lord's most valuable ways to win us to Himself is by making it crystal clear that He is for us (Romans 8:31). The more a husband knows she is for him, the more she will be able to disciple him.

6: PICK YOUR SPOTS: (Proverbs 15:1) She must learn the non-fight times to talk to her husband. She should be careful about confronting him head-on or when she is angry, an unwise and unhelpful strategy. The moment of her disappointment is not the best time to talk about what is wrong with him. She will likely say it badly, only exacerbating an already negative situation. Find a vulnerable time to speak with him. It could be when he is already talking civilly, and she feels his receptivity to what she wants to say. These are those moments when he's not as defensive, and she's not as disappointed.

7: DON'T BE MANIPULATED: (James 1:5–8) Sometimes, a husband can become defensive using manipulative tactics. Rather than owning his sin when she confronts him, he may blame, justify, or make excuses for his actions. He will do this to throw his wife off the scent of his sinful ways. If the wife is "manipulatable," she will buy what he is selling, which will cause double-mindedness. She will see his actions more clearly when she is away from him. When she is within his manipulative orbit, she loses discernment. She gets lost in his noise, and her mind becomes muddled. Some women struggle more with this than others. If she does become quickly cluttered, she needs to fixate on what is true while holding her assessments loosely (humbly). Seeking counsel may be wise. Another perspective could clear up the fog while giving her someone she can go to when her mind becomes cloudy.

8: BE A MATCHMAKER: (1 Corinthians 15:33) She should not disciple her husband alone. Though she is the primary discipler, she is not his only discipler. Part of her praying should be for a male friend who can come alongside him to help him. Build community, which could also quicken the process of sanctification. Before opening up to those closest to us, the typical person will open up more quickly to a third party they do not know.

9: FIND COMMUNITY: (Proverbs 11:14) She must have a community to help her as she helps her husband. She does not want to be alone in this endeavor. Her local church should be the best place for her to find friends to come alongside them. If she lives where that is impossible, she could seek another like-minded Christian-centric community, though it might not be a local church.

Call to Action

1. Do you love and like your husband? Some people talk about loving their spouse but not liking them. It's more than semantics; it's masking annoyances.
2. Describe your prayers for your husband. Do you have a burden for him?
3. Are you a practical, biblical example of what you want him to become? Don't be that hypocrite.
4. Are you an encourager? Explain.
5. How does your husband respond when you ask him if he thinks you are for him?
6. Do you have self-control, which governs the timing of your communication?
7. Are you easily manipulated? If so, what are your plans to change things—yourself and your marriage?
8. Who is a guy your husband may be willing to open up to and share with?
9. Who is caring for your soul?

13

Leading Practically

Every wife is equal to her husband, even though there is a call on her life to submit to him. These are not opposing truths but a biblically common-sense perspective on marriage. Hierarchy and equality do not compete but expand the possibilities for how a couple can meet their extraordinary potential, releasing the wife to practically come alongside her husband in a disciple-making capacity so that he can be the best possible leader in their union.

Equal and Different

Mable and Biff have a challenging relationship. They have been married for eleven years. What began with all the hope in the world has slowly degenerated into daily tussles. Though they are part of a local church, Biff is not engaged. It's more of a social context for him. Mable has pleaded with Biff to pursue God, but thus far, it has been to no avail. Their children are responding to his indifference and anger in various ways. Two of them internalize the disappointment they feel from their dad while the other two act out overtly, according to their personalities. Mable has tried to speak about this, but she typically botches it up, and the ensuing arguments have discouraged her.

She also does not want to overstep her bounds, which puts her in a quandary about moving forward. She read my chapter on how to lead your husband and asked if I would write more on how to do that practically. I'm glad to do that, but first, it's crucial to restate the differences between subordination in roles and equality of persons, a case I have made throughout this book. Though both partners are fully equal before God (ontology), they serve different roles (functions) as a married couple. As humans made in the image of God, there is a coequality (Genesis 1:27). If they are born again (John 3:7), there is a spiritual equality, as opposed to light and darkness (Colossians 3:9–11). Our world could not function well without hierarchy, but those structures do not mean those who serve the authorities within those structures are lesser humans than their authorities.

The husband and wife are equal human beings made in the image of God. When the wife stepped into a submissive role in the marriage, she did not leave her Imago Dei at the altar. It's not a diminishing of something but the addition of submission within the union. They are the same before God and with each other. This subordination dynamic means the wife can help (even lead in some areas) her husband to be a better person. I used the illustration of Christ as 100 percent God and 100 percent man but only loosely because any "God and God-man examples" are unique. There must be carefulness when making applications like this. Thus, the analogy is not the best. The better analogy is comparing human-to-human relationships like the employer to employee or parent to child.

The point here is that you must know how your subordinate role to your husband does not relieve you of the obligation to appropriate God's grace into your life so that you can use your unique God-giftedness to serve your husband and marriage according to your Christian leadership gifting. One of the most significant challenges for you will be to guard your heart as you think about your husband while trying to serve him in his sanctification. You will need an honest friend speaking into your life about how you think about and talk to your husband. You will not be above sinning against him. It will be a daily struggle for you if he does not change. You need a female friend, preferably at your church, willing to wound you if necessary to help you (Proverbs 27:6).

Lead by Praying

I will share with you ten practical things that will guide you in leading your husband while submitting to him, and let's begin with prayer. How often do you pray for Biff? You must pray for him. You must also say specific things to the Lord about Biff. Sometimes a wife will ask God to change her husband, and that is the extent of her prayers. That is not how Paul thought about the people he wanted to see transformed (1 Corinthians 1:4). Paul thanked God for the Corinthians. Maybe that is hard for you to do right now.

If so, you have your first leadership opportunity: ask God to give you a grateful heart for your marriage. As Mordecai told Esther, "Who knows whether you have not come to the kingdom for such a time as this?" (Esther 4:14b). You have a substantial redemptive opportunity. Paul had one with the Corinthians. Before you ask God to change your husband, ask Him to change you. If you do not fine-tune your heart before the Lord, leading Biff toward change will be hard. If you are not a grace-filled, grace-giving person, asking the Father to make your husband something you are not will be a gospel contradiction.

Lead by Encouraging

Genuine encouragement is born out of a pure heart. Moving forward with honest, authentic help will be hard if your heart struggles with Biff. Christ genuinely loved you while you were a sinner (Romans 5:8). Paul loved the Corinthians too. Don't skip this point. If your heart is not fine-tuned to God this way, you won't be able to get it tuned to Biff. Some wives have asked, "Why should I try to be an encouarement to my husband?" The answer is straightforward: motivating your husband by grace is the primary method God uses to change a person. If you want him to change, there is only one way: authentic motivation.

Paul said, "Or do you presume on the riches of his kindness and forbearance and patience, not knowing that God's kindness is meant to lead you to repentance" (Romans 2:4)? The word repentance in this verse means change. Do you want your husband to change? Of course, you do. Then how are you motivating him to change? How are you encouraging him? It cannot be negativity, anger, condemnation, shame, guilt, or other forms of frustration. If your husband is more aware of your displeasure with him, that is another area where you must lead by changing first.

Lead by Modeling

Another good assessment question is, "What kind of husband do I want?" Think about this for a minute. What if I listed a few things you might want your husband to be? Maybe you would say these things:

1. I want him to pray more.
2. I'd love for him to enjoy, encourage, and help me.
3. I want him to lead.
4. I want him to be spiritual.
5. I want him to confess his sins and ask for forgiveness.
6. I want him to be humble and teachable.
7. I want him to be more engaged with our church and the church people.
8. I want him to be kind to the children and me.

All of these things are great, and they are doable. However, there is an essential first step with desires like these: how are you modeling what you're asking him to be? If your husband lacks these good things, you should present yourself as an authentic example of being them in your home. Do not discount what a God-honoring, gospel-motivated, Christ-centered example can do for someone. You show Biff what Christ looks like through your humble modeling of Christ. Don't be that hypocritical person who demands Christlikeness without providing a Christlike example for him to follow (1 Corinthians 11:1).

How do you lead him with your prayers, encouragement, and example? Let's say you actively pray for your husband, encourage him daily, and model the standard you want him to be. I'm sure you're not doing these things perfectly, but you do them most of the time. If these things are happening, you're in the best place to gently correct him (Galatians 6:1). So now, let's look at seven more practical considerations.

1: Pick Your Spots: The best times to make loving appeals are always non-fight times. Don't try to correct your husband when you're arguing with him. The angry person is a fool, and you don't want to act like one or try to correct one (Proverbs 22:24; 29:9). Pick your spots. Leverage the good times as you try to restore him. The best approach is to do this by asking questions. Question-asking is nearly always better than statement-making. Statements can come across as accusations while question-asking acknowledges that you don't know everything about the situation. A healthy dose of self-suspicion is wise and humble during potential conflict times.

2: Think before You Speak: "Know this, my beloved brothers: let every person be quick to hear, slow to speak, slow to anger" (James 1:19). Let the wise words of James take control of your thoughts. If you do not do this, you will compound your troubles. James also said, "For the anger of man does not produce the righteousness of God" (James 1:20).

3: Ask for Forgiveness: If you blow it, which you will, you can repent. Your husband may be too stubborn to forgive you, a sad reality in too many marriages. His actions should not stop you from doing what is right. You do what you know to do whether he does it or not (Romans 12:18). You can forgive your husband in your heart even if he does not participate in active repentance. Jesus asked the Father to forgive the folks at the cross. It was not transactional repentance since they were not asking. Still, you see the heart and attitude of the Savior in that dark moment (Luke 23:34). You can follow His example, motivating you to have a forgiving heart attitude (1 Peter 2:21).

4: Honor Him before Others: Never speak angrily or unkindly about your husband to others—especially to your children. And when you sin against him by what you say, repent to all the people you dishonored before him. If your sin against Biff splashes on others because they were in the room when you did it, ask them to forgive you for your anger toward Biff.

5: Submit to Him: Submit to him as much as possible. Let him see the humble Savior in you (Philippians 2:5-10). As long as he is not asking you to sin, you should be able to submit to him. Submission does not mean you can't confront or correct him; some folks have a distorted view of love, as though it has no teeth. If someone is sinning, and you do nothing about it when you could have, that is not love.

6: Make Him a Priority: God makes you a priority. You do not deserve His attention or love, but He gives them to you anyway. The Father loved you into submission. Let this gospel truth govern your heart as you model it before your husband and family.

7: Hope in God: Finally, hope in God. Allow the Father to fill your mind with hope daily. I'm not necessarily talking about the hope that your husband will change. He may never repent. I'm talking about the eternal confidence that will enable you to endure. This hope is born in the crucible of prayer. Paul understood that the hope he found in God would buoy him through some of his most challenging seasons, which is how he framed it to the Corinthians.

> For this light momentary affliction is preparing for us an eternal weight of glory beyond all comparison as we look not to the things that are seen but to things that are unseen. For the things that are seen are transient, but the things that are unseen are eternal.
> (2 Corinthians 4:17–18)

Call to Action

1. **Pray:** What needs to change about you so that you can thank God for this opportunity you have in your marriage?
2. **Encourage:** What specific and practical ways are you an encourager to your husband?
3. **Model:** Read 1 Corinthians 13:4–7 and replace the word *love* with your name. How do you need to change as it applies to how you relate to your husband?
4. **Restore:** Are you a gentle restorer of your husband? What specific ways would support your answer?
5. **Quiet:** How does self-control characterize the use of your tongue as it relates to your husband?
6. **Forgive:** Describe your attitude of forgiveness toward your husband.
7. **Honor:** Describe how you honor him before others.
8. **Submit:** In what specific ways are you challenged to submit to him?
9. **Prioritize:** Does your husband get all of you when you're together?
10. **Hope:** How is God enabling you with His hope?

14

Over Your Head

It is common for someone to confuse their various roles within a hierarchal structure and their coequality with everyone within those structures. For example, a wife can be a sister, mother, employer, employee, church member, and citizen. She fits within all those structures, and she's equal to every person within those contexts. This perspective does not negate each other but expands the possibilities for how she can love God and others most effectively. One of the misguided roles that some women accept (or resign to) is that they are lesser than their husbands, with no responsibility to speak into their lives. This perspective can be tragic, especially if the husband walks away from God and His Word.

Help and Meet?

> And the LORD God said, It is not good that the man should be alone; I will make him an help meet for him.
>
> (Genesis 2:18, KJV)

A friend was working through these perspectives on roles and equality and wrote me the following letter:

> I struggle with the concept of a wife discipling her husband. I read most of what you have said about

this, yet I struggle with what that would look like in marriage. I believe I am to be my husband's helpmeet, under his authority, not a woman teaching a man. I believe much, if not all, of my role is to provide what he needs and wants when he needs and wants it for him to accomplish the ministry to which God has called him. What you say appeals to me, but my flesh is usually rising and trying to usurp authority over him. Will you explain more about what you mean by wives discipling their husbands?

The first place to begin is a proper understanding of her word *helpmeet*. It is one of those words we brought from our old English Bible. It should not have been one word but two. The original old English words are a help + meet. It's two words, not one. Because many folks accept the word helpmeet in modern Christian English without argument, its meaning is obscured and assumed. This perspective is unfortunate. The confusion originated in Genesis 2:18 when God said that Adam needed a helper who was suitable or complementary to him. The King James Version of the Bible says, "A help who is meet for him." Because our modern English is not the same as the 1611 English when they published the King James Bible, some people do not know what *meet* means, so they combined the two words—help and meet—as though the two were supposed to be one—helpmeet.

After the two became one, some writers modernized the non-word helpmeet to helpmate. As far as a word goes, helpmate looks and sounds much better than helpmeet, but the problem remains. The Lord initially rendered the words to communicate two different ideas as any two words do. Help refers to the person. In this case, the person helping was Eve. She was Adam's helper. Meet refers to Eve's role. She was to complement or be suitable for Adam. You could read it this way, "God is going to make a helper (Eve) who is suitable (complementary) for Adam." The made-up word "helpmeet" or the modern equivalent "helpmate" means "help-suitable," which is unnecessarily confusing. Theological precision and practical application suggest it is better to separate the words to give them their unique, accurate, and intended meanings.

The Perfect Wife

God made Adam a wife who was perfect for him. She—the helper—was suitable (meet) for Adam. Eve was not suitable for anyone else. She was perfect for Adam. Each husband has a perfectly suited wife, like a hand in a glove (Genesis 2:23). The wife's "meet role" in the marriage is a complementarian role. Christian spouses are complementarians as opposed to egalitarians. Complementary is different from the word compliment. It does not mean you praise each other, but you are perfectly suitable for each other. The husband is not better than his wife, and the wife is not better than her husband. The two complement each other perfectly. Adam needed something, and Eve had what he needed. Adam was missing a rib. Guess what? Eve was what he was looking for in a wife.

> And the rib that the LORD God had taken from the man he made into a woman and brought her to the man. Then the man said, "This at last is bone of my bones and flesh of my flesh; she shall be called Woman because she was taken out of Man.
> (Genesis 2:22–23)

Eve is not Adam. She is her own woman. She is different. Adam is not Eve. He is his own man. He is different. Both of them have missing pieces that the other person can fill. This reality is how two can become a beautiful one-flesh union. It's not like a bump added to a log, but two people who are assimilated into each other, forming a unique one-flesh union. This union means Eve was not added inferior baggage to Adam's life, but she has an essential and unique role to play in her husband's life. She is his helper who is perfectly suitable for him. Part of her suitability is her strength, which Eve needs to complement her husband. If she were a doormat or a "be seen but not heard person," she could not adequately help her husband.

Submit and Equal

> Though he was in the form of God, did not count equality with God a thing to be grasped, but emptied himself, by taking the form of a servant, being born in the likeness of men.
> (Philippians 2:6-7)

One of the concerns that my friend suggests is that she should be under her husband's authority, which is true. But submission is not all she should be to her husband. While I appreciate her humble attitude and willingness to submit to him, she must understand there is much more to how she responds to her husband. Jesus Christ took a similar position as He submitted Himself to the Father; He became a man. He willfully subordinated Himself to the Father after becoming a human being. This act of subordination does not mean He is unequal to His Father. This theological truth is what Paul was getting at in the excellent Philippians passage. This text teaches what theologians call the hypostatic union—Christ is 100 percent God and became 100 percent man. There is no contradiction here though there is much mystery.

Depending on what Christ is called upon to do determines the role He performs. His humble submission as a human does not negate His equality with the Father as 100 percent God. The wife's roles and responsibilities within the marriage covenant are analogous to what we see in Jesus. Yes, she is to subordinate herself to her husband. But, on the other hand, she is equal to her husband. You could say it this way: she is his wife in marriage and his sister in Christ. My friend only mentions one of her roles, the subordination aspect of the marriage, and while I appreciate her acknowledgment, I must call attention to the fact that she is her husband's sister in Christ. I assume both of them are believers, but even if they were not, they would be the same under God as image-bearers. Do you understand your dual and noncontradictory submission and coequal roles in your marriage?

Regrettably, a few husbands play the authority-respect card, manipulating their wives to a role of submission while not envisioning and equipping them for their coequal responsibilities. I don't sense this regarding my friend; I hope she will talk with her husband about what it would mean to envision and lead her to become a more valuable partner within the marriage. Imagine the complementing possibilities if a wife brought her unique gifts and strengths to the marriage. Nobody has more insight and intel on a husband than a wife, who has seen more aspects of his best and worst qualities than anyone else. The wise husband wants an expert to help him mature into the best possible leader, and no one has more experience with him than his wife.

Discipler-maker

To be a helper perfectly suitable for your unique husband within the framework of your unique marriage, you must grow in understanding how to be a complementary helper. An aspect of this truth means you are a teacher of your husband. Perhaps you prefer the word *discipler*. That is fine and is more accurate. Paul's language about a woman not teaching a man in the context of the local church has nothing to do with a wife's role to come alongside her husband within the home in a disciple-making capacity. Being under a person's authority should never negate loving someone enough to bring discipleship care into his life. These ideas do not contradict each other in the Bible and should not create a contradiction in your mind or marriage. If a wife is not helping her husband in his sanctification, she is not adequately fulfilling her role as a wife.

She does not have to lecture him or set up "teaching times" to bring instruction into his life while he sits at her feet. Her overall, God-given discipleship responsibilities do not begin after she walks out the door of her home, where she can only disciple others but not her husband. She should be praying about her husband, reflecting on God's Word as it applies to him, and seeking to bring reasonable care to him. If her husband is humble, he will leverage this remarkable possibility God gave him. He will perceive the wisdom of God in giving him someone who loves him so much that she wants to use her skills to serve him. The wife then becomes the perfect match that is suitable for him. Her husband will pursue her opinions, observations, and God-given wisdom.

Has your wife ever predicted what you might say or do before you said or did it? My family has done this to me many times. Afterward, I would ask, "How did you know I was going to do that?" Someone would say, "You always do [that]" because they know me better than anyone else. I would be a fool not to ask my wife to speak into my life regularly. We have multiple decades of living with each other. She knows me. In some ways, she knows me better than I do. My appeal to every wife is to prayerfully step up to the marriage plate and figure out how they can serve their husband through discipleship care. Perhaps these men are not open to this practical need in their lives. Maybe all a wife can do is pray for "doors of opportunity" to open in the future so she can bring discipleship care to him then.

A Practical Asset

Of course, a few wives err on the other side of the complementary coin as they attempt to rule over their husbands. As in most situations, there are two ditches; you want to stay out of both. You do not want to neglect the unique discipleship gift that your husband needs from you, which is a form of disrespect, dishonor, and being unloving. Disrespecting your husband while ruling over him is the other ditch at the heart of egalitarianism. Your goal is to embrace the middle narrative that releases all that God has given to you to serve your husband while not trying to dominate him. Give your husband the wisdom and insight the good Lord gave to you. You have a relationship with God. You hear from the Lord. You can discern things. You're the second set of eyes that your husband needs.

I told Lucia many years ago that I did not marry my doppelgänger. I married a uniquely different person from myself. She has things I do not possess, and I need her to give me the stuff that will assist me in becoming the most effective leader in our home. She followed up by letting me know that I needed to create a context of grace conducive to and motivating her to speak into my life. She did not want my appeal for her to care for me to collide with my stubborn refusal to resist her care. If I need her discipleship care, which I do, then making it hard for her to care for me will discourage and eventually disconnect us from this mutual marital responsibility. A wife actively and practically submitting while discipling her husband is an excellent means of grace to him.

I'm fully aware many women who are reading this will sign off on it, but their hearts will be heavy because their husbands are unwilling to cooperate with them in the mutual care of each other. I understand how discouraging that can be. These despairing women should know that their husbands are their authority, but they do not have absolute authority over them. Perhaps the most effective way to disciple these husbands is by "going over their heads." The church gives you an authority chain that is supposed to come alongside any person stuck in a non-redemptive hierarchal structure. Maybe a spiritual leader in your local church is the next authoritative person to talk to about what's happening in your marriage.

Call to Action

1. Are you actively and practically participating in your dual roles in your marriage—submission and disciple-maker?
2. What needs to change so that you can fully complement your husband, specifically how you disciple him?
3. Do you disrespect your husband? The two most common ways to disrespect him are not loving him enough to care for him and succumbing to bitterness because he is not all you had hoped for. If you disrespect your husband, how do you need to change?
4. Are you afraid of him? How does fear of man manage you when you think about speaking into his life? What is your plan to change this so you can serve him?

Conclusion

When discussing submission problems in a marriage, we should equally scrutinize the submission and leadership constructs. It's not an either/or proposition. For example, a half analysis focuses solely on the man's leadership or the wife's submission, leaving holes in the reconciliation process. We must examine both sides of the one-flesh coin. Typically, I start with the man's leadership since he's the functional leader of the home. I'm not suggesting I neglect the wife's role in submitting, but the correct starting point is vital if the goal is to help couples work through their problems.

Two Sides, One Coin

I realize submission is a hot topic within Christianity, but civil discussions can proceed if we refrain from engaging the two extreme camps participating in this debate. Those who find the idea of submission repulsive and those whose authoritarianism discolors biblical sense. Between those two groups is an ongoing, unending charitable discussion about how much a wife should submit, which always includes two talking points, not one: her responsibility to submit and a husband's requirement to lead well.

Suppose a couple is genuinely interested in working through a wife's lack of submission problem in a marriage. In that case, they must flip the coin and discuss the husband's responsibility in their one-flesh covenant. We cannot divide and isolate a wife's submission and a husband's leadership as though one does not affect the other. It is dangerous to only talk about a wife's lack of submission while not giving equal time to the husband's leadership role. If the goal is to resolve a legitimate submission problem with humility and courage, we must discuss the entire issue, not half.

No Behavioral Modification

Another instructive observation about the biblical submission issue is the lack of discussion about root causes. This incomplete approach to the problem is unfortunate because it leads to spiritual bondage at best and irreparable physical harm at worst. No Christian discipler worth their salt would hang out at the surface of any problem, especially this one. It should be evident that if a woman is not submitting to her husband, there is something under the surface of her life that is hindering her. Here are ten possibilities.

1. She is afraid to submit because of sexual abuse as a child. The lingering effect of sexual abuse can last a lifetime, requiring the utmost care from her disciplers, particularly her husband.
2. She grew up in a verbally or physically abusive family. With no template for biblical submission, her future husband must know how to create one for her, which he can do through his gentle and courageous example.
3. She struggles with habituated patterns of fear because of fallenness. This Adamic shaping influence is not her fault but an outcome of being born in Adam. Some image-bearers struggle more with fear than others. We're totally depraved but uniquely fallen.

4. She has a tiny soul (1 Thessalonians 5:14). Similar to the last point, there are folks with feebler capacities, making them susceptible to things that a sturdier-souled woman would never fear.
5. She does not know what submission looks like or how to do it. If she is similar to how I was reared, she has no template for being a wife or mother. Not growing up within a biblical family is a deficit for anyone after they marry.
6. She is a new Christian. Even an excellent desire to do right takes time and proper mentoring to grow up into Christlikeness. How long did it take you to become a mature Christian?
7. She imbibed feministic, egalitarian teaching. It can be a challenge to swap faiths. If her religion was feminism, you know that their worldview is rooted deep in the psyche, and it can take years for the washing of the Word to cleanse her from those fallen perspectives.
8. She became self-reliant. Self-sufficient people have difficulty relying—trusting, submitting—on others. Suppose her dad was a ruthless man. She learned early not to depend on him but on herself. Her ingenuity became the path to freedom, but now her husband requires her to trust and follow him.
9. She watched her dad abuse her mother and swore it would never happen to her. It's common for a child to jump from one ditch into another. In this case, she fears what might happen to her, so she doubles down on her resistance to authoritarianism.
10. She is on medication, which keeps her in cycles of erratic behavior. The majority of our culture takes meds. If you don't, you're rare. Once a person goes down the medication route, finding the proper medication will be a continuous process as the

body acclimates to the last meds, creating all sorts of soul problems.

Plus the Husband

This short list about the woman should imply a comparable list of what a husband brings into the marriage that would inhibit her from submitting to his inferior leadership. Without question, he has his baggage that gloms on to their marriage. We all do (Romans 3:23). I think about all the problems I brought into our marriage. When you mix the baggage of a man and woman into one flesh, you'll have a season of complexity, if not a lifetime. Most of the things from the previous list that apply to the woman could also apply to the man, making it wise to examine the entire one-flesh union, not just mandating a wife's submission.

If our only answer is for her to submit, we have not honored God or served the wife. We will "cliche her" by gaslighting her into behavioral submission without addressing the inner complexities of her soul or whatever complications the husband brings to the marriage. If we go down that road of forced submission without helping them, we might as well tie a millstone around the marriage and toss it into the ocean. If our first impulse is to talk about her lack of submission, it begs the question, do we want to find out why she is not submitting and his role in the marriage problems, or is the goal merely to get her to submit?

Call to Action

1. Why is it essential to address both sides of the one-flesh union when discussing submission problems?
2. Do you have a wife not submitting to you, or are you helping a couple like this? If so, will you talk comprehensively about this problem rather than just focusing on the wife?
3. What are some of the complicating factors in the wife that hinder her from submitting?
4. What are some of the complicating factors in the husband that hinder him from leading well?
5. As you address the historical shaping influences and the current heart issues, what is your practical plan to help them resolve the past, find peace in the present, and work toward a restorative future?

About the Author

Rick Thomas launched the Life Over Coffee global training network in 2008 to bring hope and help for you and others by creating resources that spark conversations for transformation. His primary responsibilities are resource creation and leadership development, which he does through speaking, writing, podcasting, and educating. In 1990 he earned a BA in Theology and, in 1991, a BS in Education. In 1993, he received his ordination into Christian ministry, and in 2000, he graduated with an MA in Counseling from The Master's University. In 2006, he was recognized as a Fellow of the Association of Certified Biblical Counselors (ACBC).

Other Books Available from Life Over Coffee

Boasting in Weakness
Centering Your Marriage on Christ
Communication
Complete Marriage
Don't Apologize
Exchange the Truth for a Lie
Help My Marriage Has Grown Cold
Identity Crisis
Local Church
Loving Me
Mad
Marriage Devotion We Are One
Politics and Culture
Parenting Devotion from Zero to Adulthood
Sex, Temptation, and Modesty
Storm Hurler
The Cyber Effect
The Talk
Wives Leading
You Decides